HONEST CONVERSATIONS
A BIBLICAL LOOK INTO EMOTIONS, FAITH, AND MARRIAGE

MATT AND ELLEN HUFFMYER

UrbanPress
PUBLISHING YOUR DREAMS

For Worldwide Distribution Printed in the USA

Urban Press
P.O. Box 8881
Pittsburgh, PA 15221-0881
+1.412.646.2780
www.urbanpress.us

Table of Contents

FOREWORD

"Another marriage book? Been there done that. Nothing seems to help. If you only knew my spouse . . . you'd understand. They're hopeless, and so is our marriage."

"Marriage should be easy. If you find the right person, your soulmate who clicks with you. then life would be blissful!"

"I'm single and cynical! I've been disappointed so many times. Relationships are a drag, so I'm done!"

"We're married, and we're okay. I can't imagine a book that would take us to okay-plus. It's ok to just be ok, isn't it?"

Does any of this sound familiar? In our years of writing, counseling, and speaking, we've heard them all. In their book, *Honest Conversations: A Biblical Look into Emotions, Faith, and Marriage*, Matt and Ellen Huffmyer tell their story that is vulnerable, transparent, and humble. As they say in their Introduction,

> The words in this book are our testimony of how God took us from a marriage that was simple, but not overly connected, to one in which we now share a deeper and richer understanding of one another and Him. These truths have also inspired us to grow in our personal faith.

There are various kinds of authors including academics, professors, zealots, and, of course, some who simply want to be able to say, "I'm a published author." But the Huffmyers are different in many ways. First, they are writing as a couple, which is difficult to do. It's far easier to write as the sole author. Second, they didn't start out with a plan to be authors; rather their goal was to better their marriage. This book isn't about theories or head knowledge. Instead, it's knowledge that has been learned and personally applied—which transforms that knowledge into wisdom. As their marriage transformed, they began to share their journey and lessons learned as they taught classes in their church and online. Eventually, they felt a desire to broaden the scope of their influence by authoring this book.

In *Honest Conversations: A Biblical Lens at Emotions, Faith and Marriage*, you will be taken on a journey that exposes you to the importance of understanding how your past experiences influence the present, both for good and bad. Matt and Ellen will explain how stress and your unrealistic expectations of self and others cause relational ruptures. They will show you the role that emotions play in relational damage and repairs. You will also learn about relational roadblocks that kill friendship and sexual intimacy. At the end of each chapter, there are biblical passages reinforcing the topic covered upon which you can reflect and further contemplate God's opinion on the chapter topic.

Finally, Matt and Ellen will share the uncommon road they took to find emotional intimacy and peace. Reading a book or attending a lecture will not change your life. Change happens when you have a successful plan and work the plan. Matt and Ellen have done and are still doing the work that builds mutual friendship and trust with one another. This book is worth your time.

Milan Yerkovich
Co-author of *How We Love*
Mission Viejo, CA
September 2025

DEDICATION

Ellen and I dedicate this book to our parents,
Bill and Gail Thornill and Lee and Caroline Huffmyer.

Both couples have been married for more than 50 years.
That's over 100 years of marriage experience between the four of
them. Amazing!

Ellen and I could not have asked for better parents. We're grateful
that the Lord chose us to be a part of their families and now to
have our own. That each of our children will have specific and
long-lasting memories with all four of their grandparents is an
added blessing.

Our parents have been a reflection of Jesus. It's our prayer that the
testimony we have written will continue both family's legacy of
commitment, service, guidance and encouragement.

Thank you, Lord Jesus, for our parents. Thank you, Lord Jesus, for
this testimony and the work You are doing in each of our lives.

★★★★★

The two greatest challenges in marriage are how we manage stress and the
expectations we have of ourselves and our spouse. The best way to handle
these stressors is to understand our emotions through a biblical lens—how
and why they operate and what we can expect when they are healed
and under the Lordship of Christ. We engage them to enable us to find
comfort and healing as we share with our spouse as the Bible says in an
"understanding way" (1 Peter 3:7). – Matt and Ellen Huffmyer

INTRODUCTION

How often have we heard on a Sunday morning that the Lord has you in the service for a reason? He wants to teach you something or minister to you in a particular area, so you are there because He has a purpose for you being there. The same is true for this book. You're reading and God has you doing so for a reason. You may be thinking, *I'm not married, so why should I read this book? Why should I care about spending time on marriage if I am single by choice or divorced or widowed?*

We have also heard it said that when we talk about marriage, we are only speaking to half the Church. We initially agreed with that statement until the Lord said something different to us. *Are we not also leaving half the people out by not being intentional about discussing marriage?*

The Lord has a purpose for presenting this material to you regardless of your marital status. Scripture says that marriage is a picture of the relationship between Christ and the Church. That being true, having an understanding of the marriage relationship is important for you for at least two reasons. We all have developed patterns in how we relate with each other. We all have wounds from the past, usually inflicted through those relationships closest to you, that the Lord desires to heal.

We think you will agree that we learn a lot about ourselves through relationships. You may not currently be married, but you are a part of the bride of Jesus. It is our prayer that you will continue to read, so that you can experience much-needed healing for yourselves, your spouses and with the Lord. And if you aren't married now, perhaps you will be married or remarried one day. The time to prepare for that is now, not right before you get married. And we should all have the goal of upholding marriage as an institution regardless of our own marital status.

Being emotionally and spiritually naked and unashamed was God's original intention for Adam and Eve in the Garden of Eden. He wants that to be the case not only for our personal relationship with Him, but with others as well—especially with our marriage partner. Learning about marriage will allow you to be more effective in your ministry. The tools provided through this book will help all of us deepen our understanding and our faith.

There is a scene in Disney's movie *Jungle Book* in which vultures sit on a branch asking, "What do you want to do?" If you have seen the movie, perhaps you can see them shrugging their shoulders and responding, "I don't know. What do you want to do?" (with more shrugging). The conversation continues but repeats the "what do you want to do?" question, followed by a "now don't start that again!" comment. This scene is memorable for us in how it regularly plays out in our married life, complete with the shrugs.

Matt : Do you want to go to a movie?

Ellen: I don't know. What do you want to see?

Matt: I think I picked last time. Anything you pick would be great!

Ellen: No seriously. I don't really care what we watch, you?

Matt: Nope

This is a real conversation that has played out in our relationship on many occasions. However, there are many other conversations that also occur in our marriage. Perhaps you can also relate:

Ellen: Are you ok?

Matt: Yes, I'm fine.

Ellen: Are you sure? What's going on?

Matt: Yes. I'm fine. (plays on his phone)

Ellen interprets silently "Is he really okay?"

Ellen (verbally): I don't believe you. There's more going on than you're telling me. Why won't you talk with me?

This is typical of how we have engaged with one another over the years. It's not the subject matter of the conversation that's important, but the process we go through in the conversation. How we engage with others feels normal because we have done so on countless occasions. When the person we are with shares a different perspective than we have, conflict can, and often does, occur in marriage—and outside of it.

We think our spouse is the one who isn't the normal one, sometimes labeling them as *wrong* or *stubborn* or *misguided*. We tend to look to blame and defend our "rightness" when conflict with them occurs. In our mind, we make sense. If the other person is wrong, then the best thing to do is to immediately correct them, right?

We soon discover that we are more like our spouses in how we react and respond to each other than we are different. We will see why our emotions are more logical and rational than we currently believe. We eventually understand that being right is not all it's cracked up to be. "Being right" keeps the wedge lodged into the divide of our relationship.

Paul gave us simple advice that's easy to read but difficult to follow: "Let your conversation be gracious and attractive so that you will have the right response for everyone" (Colossians 4:6). Our goal in communicating with our spouse is to understand and know them more intimately and accurately. How we communicate either helps or hurts our relationship. And our history, usually not the one with our partner, plays an important part in how we communicate. It can be attractive and encourage intimacy, or it can help contribute to despair and a pattern of misunderstanding and anger.

This isn't a book about everything you do wrong, or everything your spouse says you do wrong. It's not about what you think they do wrong. The Lord has asked Ellen and I to share a much-needed message that we believe is from His heart and that is that we are made in His image. Jesus has given us our primary relationships as a picture of the ultimate fellowship we will have with Him. He created needs in us that require us to seek out others for them to be met.

When Adam and Eve were created, they were naked and unashamed. Being naked or intimate is about much more than sex. Intimacy requires that we understand emotions, good and bad. Once we understand those, we will need to communicate them effectively with others. Understanding our emotional needs through identifying and experiencing our emotions will not only draw us closer to each other but ultimately to Him.

Jesus has made us have a need for intimacy with others,

ultimately pointing us to our need for intimacy with Him. For some, that is found and expressed in a marriage covenant. Jesus loves us all. What's more, there's no condemnation in Christ Jesus. All of us come into relationships with concerns, distractions, and stress that, at times, can be overwhelming. They all play out most intensely in our closest relationships. That leads to an unusual dynamic where we can treat those we don't know better than our primary relationships. Ironically, the very relationships which are most precious to us often add the most stress and often lead us away from intimacy.

It is our prayer that you will find some relief and perspective. The words in this book are our testimony about how God took us from a marriage that was simple, but not especially connected, to one in which we share a deeper and richer understanding of one another and Him. These truths have also inspired us to grow in our personal faith.

This book will encourage you to learn about your emotions and learn from your emotions. If you're like me [Matt],this may be your first time to learn and experience them. For others, this will be a needed perspective check to change some patterns of thought and behavior. Doing so lessens the stress you desire to relieve. It will challenge long-standing notions about your thought life and behavior that you have. For that reason, this book won't always be an easy or comfortable read. If you allow Him, however, God can use your discomfort to get your attention.

This also isn't a book to sit down and read from cover to cover in a day or two. Read a chapter and spend some time engaging the tools and digging deeper into sections that hold your interest. God did that with us and now the intimacy and understanding in our relationship have never been better. We eagerly anticipate that He will do the same for you.

What would happen if you were to view your spouse, not as a problem to be solved, but as a friend and ally, one who is interested in hearing and understanding your joy and pain? What would happen if you were to go through life confident that your spouse is a lover of your soul? This produces a feeling of trust, not just that wonderful feeling we have when we stand on our wedding day and say I do, but the day-in-day-out emotional bond that can develop and grow over time. Would that perspective change your marriage?

It is our prayer that you find the means to a transformed

relationship in the following pages and the comfort and peace that comes with a better understanding of your emotional needs and those of your lifetime partner.

Matthew and Ellen Huffmyer
Pittsburgh, PA
September 2025

CHAPTER 1

GETTING STARTED

Motivational speaker Zig Ziglar said that when we are communicating with an audience, we should tell them what we are going to tell them, tell them, and then tell them what we told them. That is the strategy we have determined to use to write our testimony. Many agree that marriage is under attack in our culture. Our greatest challenge in marriage is not our culture, but inside our marriages.

The two greatest challenges in marriage are how we manage stress and the expectations we have of ourselves and our spouse. The best way to handle stress and expectations is to understand our emotions—how and why they operate and what we can expect when they are healed and under the Lordship of Christ—through a biblical lens. We engage them to find comfort and healing through sharing with our spouse.

Our goal is to have a biblical understanding of emotions: why

1

and how we have them, and how to learn to respond to them—or despite them. Having emotions does not demonstrate a lack of faith or substandard spirituality. Consider the example of King David, a man after God's own heart. Rather than pulling away from or hiding his emotions, he poured them out to God.

We sometimes do the opposite. We don't like to entertain their existence or allow them room in our mind. We know we can impact or modify them, but we often don't control when they happen. Quite simply, emotions are not sinful. We see in Scripture that God is in fact emotional and yet perfect. Therefore, we are emotional because we are made in His image. Genesis 1:27 states, "So God created man in his own image, in the image of God, male and female He created them."

From a human perspective, all emotions have a positive and negative side. Jesus shows us that it is possible to be emotional and not sin. We sometimes allow the two to be connected, but emotion in and of itself is not sin as Scripture demonstrates. Ephesians 4:26 says in your anger do not sin. We will see that the Bible refers to emotions more than salvation, sin, or other common Christian theological topics. We say that not to elevate emotions to a status more important than salvation, but to show that emotions merit our attention because they are part of who God made us to be. Emotions are the warning lights on the dashboard of our lives. They give us a heads up as to what is going on in our souls and minds. Therefore, paying attention to them is of the utmost importance. They can lead us to the nakedness and intimacy God desires for us. He teaches us about intimacy with Him through intimacy with others.

We have read books, attended conferences, and listened to or watched sermons about relationships. We never made the commitment, however, to invest time and effort into applying the principles so they would become part of our unconscious behavior. What's more, the tools we used addressed our behaviors but did not dig deep into the root cause of the emotional triggers that were causing the behavior. Because of that, we failed to make any lasting change or progress in our marriage.

You may wonder what caused us to change. The answer is simple: We wanted more and found that these principles worked. We were bummed out and burned out, simply going through the motions. Although our intentions were good, nothing ever changed.

We did not experience rough patches in our marriage but, in truth, we were missing out on the good aspects of a healthy, Christ-centered relationship. We were missing out on our calling to help one another other grow closer to each other and the Lord.

We can present these practices to you now because we have lived them. The material, questions, and comments we will share are simple. Applying the principles, however, will take time, effort, transparency, and faith. Answering the questions these principles create for yourself and hearing your spouse's responses likely won't be easy or comfortable. We have found that many resist or ignore their feelings. Especially at first, the temptation to resist will be strong. We have all spent most of our lives learning how to relate to others. Anticipate these challenges and don't allow them to stop you from change. Life does not happen without the need to have a "do over" from time to time. Years ago, our mentors reminded us of the following phrase that needs to describe a common comment between married couples: "I'm sorry, I was wrong. Will you forgive me?"

We are excited to boast about what the Lord has taught us. These principles work in marriage or our other day-to-day relationships. The more time and effort we put in, the more change and understanding we will experience. As you read, many of the assumptions you carry from the past will be challenged. Understanding our emotions changes our behaviors which becomes more natural as we grow. We create new techniques and attitudes that are much more effective. If you stick with it, you will experience not only increased intimacy and an enhanced relationship with your spouse, but the same will be true in your relationships with others and the Lord.

Our conversations started *at* each other but in time became conversations *with* each other. There were many sources of inspiration for us. The first is a faithful couple, Milan and Kay Yerkovich, whose "How We Love" ministry started it all for us. Milan and Kay are beautiful examples of people who are willing to step out in faith and transparently share their journey. We also want to thank the pastors and leadership team at Allegheny Center Alliance Church on the Northside of Pittsburgh. Their faithful preaching and service to a diverse community have inspired many aspects of this message.

One of the most important is to engage others who are different from us. Our purpose is not to be right, change someone, or to win a debate or argument. We learn so much by engaging with those with different experiences. We also can dispel the false assumptions we have in our minds about others when we truly listen to understand them. Thank you, ACAC, for giving us the platform where we could learn to do that.

There could be a temptation to look at some of the principles in this book and on the surface see "Jesus plus," meaning that it may seem we are supplementing biblical truth with the secular. In fact, that was the impression we had initially as well. However, what we are writing is to show that understanding non-biblical concepts as truth in no way minimizes the truth of Scripture. The problem is when we selectively use Scripture to justify a predetermined conclusion.

We don't believe God has tasked us with sharing any new or original thoughts, but He has challenged us to think differently about what we know to add some additional verifiable truth into the mix of our understanding. All those mentioned above have helped us learn how to see others through His eyes instead of our own. When this happens, the joy is indescribable, as is His grace. In truth, we all need healing and understanding. Be encouraged, you will find that in this book.

Our Heavenly Father is wildly crazy in love with you. If you have not sought a personal relationship with Him, this journey to understand your past and your emotional self that God created will help you better understand yourself and Him. He loves you and can't wait for you to be on this journey. Our God is an emotional God who is willing to do and has done anything and everything to be in relationship with us. He is reaching out with His big, strong, loving arms and saying, "I see you. You're important to Me. I love you." He wants to be your comfort.

We often struggle to see that, and those struggles hinder how we see and understand Him. Be still and know that He is a God of comfort who wants to help you rest in Him.

> Praise be to the God and Father of our Lord Jesus Christ, the Father of compassion and the God of all comfort, who comforts us in all our troubles, so that we can comfort those in any trouble with the comfort we ourselves receive from God (2 Corinthians 1:3-4).

When we started this journey, we could not remember much from our past and thus could not see any relevance or link to the present. We both had loving parents who provided stable homes. However, the Lord brought back memories of actions and reactions that shaped the dynamics of our marriage relationship. It was a blessing that we shared this journey of discovery together. Someone said it is rare that both of us would come together in the way that we have. That is a powerful acknowledgement from outside of our relationship that what we are about to share is effective.

The first step in healing is to recognize the pattern and the need for relationships. The second is to be willing to address the reasons behind the reactions that we have in those relationships. We will start by looking at the need for relationships through the lens the Bible provides. So, let's get started.

MARRIAGE MATTERS TOOLS FOR CHAPTER 1

We have developed a set of exercises to provide tangible tools and to encourage a perspective change. The more time you spend seeking and being open to a different perspective, the greater the blessing this journey will be. We will start our focus with non-verbal listening, then move to reflective listening. The final set of tools will revolve around listening to understand and speaking to be known.

Non-verbal listening sounds easy, right? All you must do is zipper your mouths and listen. You may even need a prop like someone holding a Kleenex box to serve as a reminder of who is talking and who should be listening. The goal of this initial exercise is to take two minutes to talk about one subject. The focus for the speaker is to stick to only one topic. The listener should just keep quiet and encourage and affirm the speaker. *You don't have to agree with a person to affirm their feelings.* It would be appropriate at this point for the listener to say things, like, "Tell me more" while offering supportive remarks like, "That's understandable, that makes sense." Remember, the actions or reactions of others do not excuse you from your responsibility to respond as Jesus would have you do.

So here goes. We want you to think about something that gets you excited. It could be a hobby or something that happened recently. Keep things light and fun for now. When you start this conversation, face each other so you can look each other in the eye and if you're comfortable doing so, engage in some physical but non-sexual touching. That might be holding hands or placing your hand on the other's shoulder or knee. It could be just having your legs touch sitting across from each other. If doing this is uncomfortable, always defer to and respect the person with the most restrictions. Then we want you to in two minutes to

1. Name your topic.
2. Start sharing details about the topic.
3. Keep the focus on the speaker—for two minutes.

An example here might help.

"For me, one of the positive things that I [Matt] am excited about is my model train hobby. When I was young, my father put up an HO scale train for Christmas. I enjoyed that time so much that I knew when I bought my own home, I would want to do the same. We bought our first house, but it was not big enough to have a train layout. I always hoped that someday we would move, and I would be able to have the space."

"Ellen, you always knew that model trains were something that was important to me. As the years went by it became more obvious that moving to a bigger house was not what God had planned for us. That meant when I thought about trains, I was disappointed because it looked like that was never going to happen for me. The one place we could have the platform built was not ideal because we regularly would get water in our basement. (You'll be glad to know the water issues have been solved.) I so appreciate what happened next because I was bemoaning the fact once again that I was not going to be able to have a train platform when you said why not put it in the garage?

"I, of course, rejected that idea initially but then I began to think. It means so much to me that you support me in my desire to have a train platform. The more I thought about it, the more delighted I was. Now that I have started the platform, I get to daydream and go back in my mind to a place of fun in my youth, relaxation, family, and all the positive emotions that Christmas brings.

"Your support of me in this has made all the difference. Even when you question what I am doing on the platform now that it is being built, I know that you are engaging with me, which makes me even more determined to build it well. I know too that building it means that I sometimes disappear to the garage. For me, that time is quite beneficial as I listen to worship music or even sometimes the Christmas music of my youth regardless of the month. Thank you so much for encouraging me."

Now it is your turn. Put the book down (temporarily) and reach out to your spouse. Be the listener and then reverse the roles.

★★★★★

These next follow-up questions are important. The reason they are relevant is because you want to establish a baseline to determine where you and your spouse are in your communication. We can't get to somewhere new if we don't know where we are starting.

7

The goal initially is also to have a positive experience through this exercise about something fun. After completing this exercise a few times, returning to it and selecting more challenging topics will be the next step into honest conversations about your marriage. We have left some space under these questions to provide an area where you can journal, but you may want to maintain a separate journal to include more of what you are learning. Writing can help you clarify what you are thinking and feeling. Having a written record will help you remember more effectively.

EVALUATE YOUR PROGRESS

1. What did you learn about your spouse?

2. What did you learn about your own emotions and perspective?

3. Are you motivated to do this again with another topic?

DIGGING DEEPER INTO CHAPTER 1

At the end of each chapter, we will also provide a word and some additional Bible verses for consideration. There are a lot of Scripture passages in each chapter. Choose one of the verses below or look up each reference. Ask the Lord to search your heart. He knows you better than anyone. He wants you to dig deeper to better understand. Record your thoughts in your journal.

This chapter's Word search is

delight

Psalm 37:4

Psalm 37:23

Isaiah 61:10

Zephaniah 3:17

CHAPTER 2

RECOGNIZING THE NEED
FOR RELATIONSHIPS

There was a television show hosted by Bob Ross which aired from 1983 to 1994 on the Public Broadcasting Station. Bob loved to paint scenes of mountains and landscapes that inspired him from his youth. If you have not experienced "The Joy of Painting," we would encourage you to look him up on YouTube. At the beginning of the show, the colors listed on the bottom of the screen begin to scroll while his smooth, uplifting voice introduces that show's masterpiece. Bob would talk about the use of Prussian Blue, Magic White, and other colors on each show, but every time they are mixed in such a way that ends in a unique masterpiece. Marriages are like his show and paintings. We all have common colors such as our circumstances and perspectives. Recognizing and learning more about each of these colors individually helps understand who we are and how we interact.

God has given us our canvas. We are masterpieces created by the Master's hands. The images Bob Ross creates are profound and complex just like we are. We have been given an opportunity in marriage to reveal and merge the image of God placed in each one of us and our spouse. The colors that are already on the canvas, our history and perspectives, will have an impact on how we use the ones we are about to apply. They help create details that are not on the brush when it is applied. We can mix the colors of our histories and perspectives to make something new, healthy and exciting.

A conversation with a friend about Bob Ross led to the question, "Have you ever tried to mix the colors like he does?" Yes, but they just all end up one blob of a color. The good news is that God is the Master Artist. He can help us mix our history and our present to make a beautiful, unique picture. What's more, He invites our participation. When we look to Him, He will reveal all the individual details that seem to just appear with a few strokes of the brush. There are 31 seasons of the "Joy of Painting." Our relationships, like painting, take time and practice. As we continue to paint, the individual strokes reveal the beauty of what God is creating.

The Lord provides much-needed comfort and growth through primary relationships. The marriage relationship is an earthly picture of our ultimate relationship with Jesus. Part of His image in us is that we are made for relationships. Genesis 2:18 states, "The LORD God said, "It is not good for the man to be alone. I will make a helper suitable for him." We also see God Himself is relational as He states in Genesis 1:26. "Let **us** make mankind in **our** image, in **our** likeness" (emphasis added). We know that we are made in the image of the Father, Son, and Holy Spirit. Relationship was not created, it is part of the very nature of God and will exist through eternity, and therefore is and will be an important part of our identity.

There is no greater priority than our relationship with the Lord. The entire Bible is God's plan for redemption so that He can have a relationship with us. God knew that man being alone is not good, even though Adam was made perfect in the Garden and in his relationship with God. In effect, we need relationships because that is who God is and how God designed us. Life without relationships is not good according to God Himself. Therefore, we need relationships for life to be good and meaningful. The word in the original language for *good* means *in harmony with God*. Our earthly relationships point us toward God. As we lean into our relationships, we find many other benefits they bring to a fuller life.

1. *We encourage one another.* We all have experienced swings in our perspectives, moods, and preferences. Some days we feel on top of the mountain. The next day, we're down in a ditch. We all need regular encouragement, like sunlight, air, or water. In 1 Thessalonians 5:11, Paul wrote, "Therefore encourage one another and build one another up, just as you are doing." Part of God's plan for relationships is that they will provide us with that much needed encouragement. Matt and I [Ellen]will text each other during the day. I can let him know by sending him an SOS in a moment when I am feeling discouraged. Even him saying, "I'm sorry to hear that" or "that's rough" can help gain much-needed perspective, and let me know someone cares.

2. *We protect each other.* Life presents challenges where we need others to keep us safe emotionally, spiritually and physically. Ecclesiastes 4:12 says, "Though one may be overpowered, two can defend themselves. A cord of three strands is not quickly broken." Our spouse becomes the earthly comforter God uses. We both have broken places in our histories. Those broken places create weaknesses. Jesus is that third strand that strengthens the other two and we become an unbreakable cord.

3. *We deepen our understanding of intimacy.* Our spouse choosing us daily as their lifelong companion is cool. Just as in our relationship with Jesus, relationships are much more than logical choices. Experiencing the emotions that result from those choices is much better. How many of us want to hear something like, "Honey, I want to go on a date with you because I'm obligated to make good on the choice I made 30 years ago?" Although that is factually true, those words don't exactly say anything positive about what is happening now. The facts leave out the

positive feelings of joy and excitement of spending time with your spouse. Facts are more superficial or surface. Feelings allow us to take steps towards true emotional intimacy.

4. *We help each other grow.* First Peter 4:8 states, "Above all, love each other deeply, because love covers over a multitude of sins." It is easy to point the finger of blame at ourselves or others. It is more difficult to love unconditionally. Healthy relationships require that we put the finger of blame away and extend the hand of grace. Relating with our spouse gives us an opportunity to practice that. Relationships give us an opportunity to see other aspects of God that we would not necessarily see only looking at ourselves. We can learn about love, grace, mercy, forgiveness, and so much more. We learn to give and receive grace and forgiveness in a way we would want others to give us. The Lord has forgiven us, and we can then begin to understand how we can forgive others.

Praise be to the God and Father of our Lord Jesus Christ, the Father of compassion and the God of all comfort, who comforts us in all our troubles, so that we can comfort those in any trouble with the comfort we ourselves receive from God. For just as we share abundantly in the sufferings of Christ, so also our comfort abounds through Christ. If we are distressed, it is for your comfort and salvation; if we are comforted, it is for your comfort, which produces in you patient endurance of the same sufferings we suffer. And our hope for you is firm, because we know that just as you share in our sufferings, so also you share in our comfort (2 Corinthians 1:3-7).

Paul later writes in verses 8 and 11 that part of achieving that comfort is through sharing with each other and prayer. We will share a lot of Scripture throughout the book. However, the challenge is to share and apply the truth as is stated, not use it to support a predetermined perspective. Is it appropriate to use concepts from the study of psychology to enhance our understanding of what the

Scripture demands? We believe the answer is yes. We use all kinds of technology to make our outreach and Sunday morning experience attractive and effective. We study the interpretations of others as we engage the truth of Scripture using footnotes and commentaries.

MARRIAGE MATTERS TOOLS FOR CHAPTER 2

This next section will seem familiar because you will continue to practice non-verbal listening. We urge you not to skip over it. This practical application will make all the difference in retaining and applying this potentially new perspective. This time let's up the ante. Rather than something fun like a hobby, the topic should be related to your relationship

1. Talk about one thing that most impresses you about your spouse.

2. What are two or three positive emotions that you feel when you think about your spouse?

3. The goal is also to proactively produce a positive experience from your relationship through this exercise.

EVALUATE YOUR PROGRESS

1. What did you learn about your spouse?

2. What did you learn about your own emotions and perspective?

3. Are you willing to do this again, this time discussing another topic?

DIGGING DEEPER INTO CHAPTER 2

This chapter's Word search is
comfort

2 Corinthians 1:4

Isaiah 40:1

Genesis 24:67

Psalm 147:3

SECTION 1

YOUR PAST IMPACTS YOUR PRESENT

Your mental, emotional, and spiritual responses are based upon the experiences you have had since before birth and throughout the course of life. You go back into your past to help you understand the present and your responses to current events. You often hear that looking back in this way is not consistent with biblical directives. There are even passages where focusing on the past is considered a sin. The difference in what we are suggesting is that you go back to understand and grow in the present.

Scripture's primary purpose is to show God's plan for relationship with His people. One of the regular admonitions in Scripture is to remember. We are going to show biblically that the very essence of who you were created to be means going back into your past so you can more fully understand who and where you currently are. We have learned that our past has impacted and continues to impact our present. You may not have specific memories of how that occurred, but the Lord will show you as you reflect and are ready to receive them.

We see in Genesis that, even though Adam lived in a perfect creation and direct fellowship with God, the Lord declared Adam being alone without Eve was not a good thing. It is interesting that the Lord established human primary relationships in the Garden of Eden prior to sin entering the world. That indicates that our one-on-one relationships are vital for our time here on earth, so much so that primary relationships were needed even when things were perfect. The Lord knew that an important part of a perfect relationship with Him would need to include others.

Many of us came into our marriages with an ideal image of the perfect marriage. Perhaps we even idolized our spouse. Adam was astounded when Eve arrived in the perfection of the Garden. The expectations coming into marriage are high as well but, quite frankly, they don't have a chance of being realized. Milan and Kay Yerkovich wrote in their book, "I have never felt this frustrated by anybody before. Only my spouse makes me feel this way, it must be his or her fault" (Yerkovich, p. 8).

Going back again to the Garden, we see the tendency to deflect our responsibility right after sin entered the world. Adam blamed Eve, and Eve blamed the serpent. Deflection contributes to division. Adam and Eve went from being naked and unashamed to covered and ashamed. Their level of intimacy changed. The most significant consequence of their sin was the breaking of the relationship between humans and God. It is also significant that things drastically changed in the relationship that God had in mind between the man and woman.

In Genesis 3, we read,

> God said to the woman, "I will make your pains in childbearing very severe; with painful labor you will give birth to children. Your desire will be for your husband, and he will rule over you." To Adam he said, "Because you listened to your wife and ate fruit from the tree about which I commanded you, 'You must not eat from it,' "Cursed is the ground because of you; through painful toil you will eat food from it all the days of your life. It will produce thorns and thistles for you, and you will eat the plants of the field. By the sweat of your brow you will eat your food until you return to the ground, since from it you were taken; for dust you are and to dust you will return" (Genesis 3:16-19).

This passage frames the significant challenges we experience in our relationships. The Lord addressed Adam and Eve and referenced their important roles that existed before sin entered the world. Even though there is no evidence that Eve had children before she ate the apple, her body was created to give birth. Childbirth and hard work were two of many roles created for us, all pre-existing to sin. We have many other roles and responsibilities in how we live, respond, react, love, and minister. Scripture gives us both a big picture perspective along with specific tools to help us overcome relationship challenges that are our responsibility to address.

Scripture will show us the following:

1. Understand who we are in Jesus and how we were created.

2. Remember and acknowledge our past.

3. Listen to understand, not to change or critique.

4. Speak to be known, not to blame.

We will spend the rest of the book exploring those four topics.

CHAPTER 3

UNDERSTANDING WHO YOU ARE

The Bible is specific that human beings are uniquely created by God for relationship with Him and each other. He knew us before He started knitting us together physically in the womb. That knitting includes our heart, mind, and personality. All must exist in the womb for Him to know us at that point of our development. Therefore, it is appropriate as we seek understanding to consider back that far.

For years I [Matt] have been quiet and much happier being alone than spending time with others. I once told the Lord that I was happy being behind the scenes in ministry and that I would never need to be "out front." I was neither the life of the party nor the person who others were attracted to when I entered a room. I was fine with that, believing that was the way I was made. Being in social situations caused stress. Like a crock pot, it took me some time to warm up in these situations. This is not to say that I never had fun, but I was much more comfortable being alone. Even though I felt energized by the end of a social event, I still struggled to initiate conversations with people I did not know.

I also had a hard time acknowledging when others would say something positive about my ability, performance, or personality even though I was blessed to have a family that was involved in my life. I also was blessed to have parents who encouraged my Christian faith, but still, *this is who I am*, or so I thought.

The truth of who we are and our perceptions of our own value don't always coincide. There often is a gap between what the Bible says and our experience or perspective of who we are. I grew up learning the truth found in the Scriptures, but the truth of what I learned did not fuel my experience. Jeremiah 1:5 is clear: "Before I formed you in the womb I knew you, before you were born I set you apart; I appointed you as a prophet to the nations." I knew Jeremiah was correct, but I was unable to see how it applied to me. I could not see myself through a biblical lens.

Psalm 139:13-18 builds on what the Lord knew about us even before He started creating us.

"For you created my innermost being; you knit me together in my mother's womb. I praise you because I am fearfully and wonderfully made; your works are wonderful, I know that fully well. My frame was not hidden from you when I was made in the secret place, when I was woven together in the depths of the earth. Your eyes saw my unformed body; all the days ordained for me were written in your book before one of them came to be. How precious to me are your thoughts, God! How vast is the sum of them! Were I to count them, they would outnumber the grains of sand when I awake, I am still with you."

Our Creator crafted us individually, and He did the same with our spouse. One of the reasons we are different from our spouse is for the purpose of challenging one another to become more like Jesus. If we were both the same, we would not be able to challenge each other to grow or change. Although we have our limits, God uses our spouses and others as a vehicle to uncover what was made in secret. That secret place God is revealing is mostly in our experiences we don't remember, defined as implicit memories. He uses others and challenges us to grow and have a better understanding of our own hearts and how they were shaped and molded through our interactions with others over the course of our lives. Our application of the principles we are sharing sheds light on those secret places we previously could not see.

One of the initial concerns we hear when we teach this is that a person does not have many or any memories to understand and apply these principles. That isn't a problem, for we thought the same thing. But those memories are stored in our brains. The Lord will reveal them when we ask and are ready. Sin and our past make getting to intimacy and self-knowledge more difficult. With help from the Holy Spirit, we have all the tools we need. Our spouse is the one who is positioned most strategically to shine a light on those memories. There is plenty of material available in our minds to explore over our lifetime. Psalm 139 numbers them as grains of sand.

Ellen and I have spent all our lives involved in a church. We knew intellectually that we were valued by God but didn't experience or process the value in a way that would change our perceptions of ourselves. Easily repeating in our minds what we learned at church and what we heard from family did not translate into our daily experience. The conversations with close friends also were surface at best. We thought we understood who we were and for the most part we were happy with that, but the Lord had a different perspective and plan. Good or bad, we never really understood the patterns that had developed of how we related with each other.

Let's continue our search for insight on this because the Bible gives us excellent advice about understanding who we are. Even though we didn't initially understand, the Lord used our relationship with each other to teach us.

First, honest confession and prayer lead to understanding then to healing. Our spouse is our closest neighbor. Through confession or talking with others, they and the Lord will give us a clearer understanding of who we are. James 5:16 states, "Therefore confess your sins to each other and pray for each other so that you may be healed. The prayer of a righteous person is powerful and effective." We now know through the study of psychology and biology that the brain can heal physically through positive long-term conversations.

God revealed this truth in His Word long before we figured it out through human study.

Second, honesty about ourselves to ourselves and with each other changes our self-perspective or self-image. We often have trouble seeing our flaws because we're so used to them. They feel normal because we learned them and reinforced them over many years. They were influenced though by the bonding or the lack thereof we had with others. I [Ellen] saw Matt's lack of emotions as an unwillingness to dive deeper. I [Matt] saw Ellen's persistence as emotionally immature. I [Matt] rarely communicated what was really going on and Ellen returned to the same issues. Our assumptions about ourselves and each other were not accurate.

We see as we share our journey that many of our assumptions were wrong. A proper relationship can help us see ourselves as we are. We needed to apply the truth found in Ephesians 4:25. "Therefore, having put away falsehood, let each one of you speak the truth with his neighbor, for we are members of one another." This is also a tool to help us see who we are in a positive sense, so we don't diminish the gifts and positive aspects of who God made us to be.

Third, we develop patterns that subconsciously guide how we interact. As we mature, we repeat the same patterns and discussions. Those patterns became our "truth." We can perceive ourselves to be factually accurate (stating the truth that we know) while not being fully honest. The bad news is that negative patterns lead to unnecessary challenges. The good news is acknowledging the tendency for us to repeatedly operate in those same patterns is useful in healing and transformation. Developing positive patterns through diligence and discipline reverses the downward spiral and negative impact of our past and helps us focus our eyes on Jesus. Our spouse runs the race with us and provides encouragement.

Fourth, our false assumptions and our lack of understanding contributed to the struggle in our relationship because we were undisciplined. Paul wrote in 1 Corinthians 9:27 (NIRV), "But I discipline my body and keep it under control." The patterns of the past did not work well when stress and emotions arose between us. It took discipline and a lot of practice to be intentional in changing those patterns. We had to unlearn years of having done things a certain way. It was far easier to default into what we had learned in the past, even when deep down we knew the results would not change.

Fifth, once our new discipline started to impact change, seeing the changes in each other motivated us to reach out proactively and do more. Those good works built positive patterns. We found that our different strengths and weaknesses complemented each other and did not need to be a source of conflict. Hebrews 10:24-25 says, "And let us consider how we may spur one another on toward love and good deeds, not giving up meeting together, as some are in the habit of doing, but encouraging one another—and all the more as you see the Day approaching."

We see in this passage how our relationships can move us in a positive direction rather than cause us to spiral downward as we achieve the same flawed or less-than-ideal results. Hebrews 12:1 says, "Therefore, since we are surrounded by such a great cloud of witnesses, let us throw off everything that hinders and the sin that so easily entangles. And let us run with perseverance the race marked out for us." What weight is hindering you right now?

God uses our time confessing with others to accomplish a few things. Spending time talking about or even writing so others can understand helps in our own forgiveness and healing process. Part of the process of repentance is walking away from past behavior. Seeking knowledge that includes the root causes of those behaviors improves our ability to successfully change them. By doing so, we have laid the foundation of understanding over the last few years so we can have honest conversations. It took time to get to the point where we could share appropriately and in full honesty.

We did not have a lot of memories when we first started that would help lead to productive, honest conversations and understanding, so we asked the Lord to show us. By revealing and helping us apply these five biblical principles, He provided what we needed. And He revealed them one at a time so that we were not overwhelmed. We would not be ready or able to handle it if the Lord did a full dump and opened up everything simultaneously. We should not do a full dump on our spouse for the same reason. Let's take that next step and believe that the Lord will provide what we need to remember and move on.

MARRIAGE MATTERS TOOLS FOR CHAPTER 3

Let's go back to Hebrews Chapter 12 to ask what's weighing you down personally. Let's keep the topic about you, the reader, not your spouse. Examples of what to talk about could be: a tough time at work or with a friend. Maybe your relationship with the Lord is not where you want to be. You may be able to recognize a past or present experience that is holding you back—or maybe not. It's okay if you can't. Go to the Lord in prayer and ask Him to help you. You may not initially hear an answer. That is also okay. Keep pursuing Him.

We still want to use the non-verbal communication skills from our previous tools. The temptation here as the speaker might be to pile on, blame and try to solve all your challenges all at once. Stick with one topic. As the topics become more about the deeper relationship challenges, the temptation for the listener will be to try to fix, minimize, or defend. We will outline in future chapters tools that show a different way of looking at how to effectively lighten the load and bring comfort to one another. For now, the goal is only to understand. Staying in that place won't always be easy.

We will give you an example but then take some time and write some of your thoughts below or in your own journal. I [Ellen] had a friend recently ask me what I thought were the sin problems in her family. Good friend or not, this is not how I would choose to conduct a conversation—telling another person what is wrong with her or her family. I identified what I wanted to say to her. I would not normally consider approaching a conversation like this. I reminded her that she had asked, and I really hoped it would be okay. She thanked me for my insight.

In this situation, as the listener, God blessed Ellen because the conversation sparked some great thoughts for her as well. "What came next, to me, was surprising. Having had this conversation with another, I decided to ask God what my sin pattern was. God answered me almost instantaneously: my sin pattern is one of complaining."

"I praised God in that moment, thanking Him for revealing that to me. "Yes, Lord", I said. "I accept this and I'm sorry. What's next?" God said to me, about as clearly as I have ever heard Him,

"No, we are going to stay here a little while."

My friend had asked for accountability from me. In turn, I recognized the need to do that for myself and turned to God for answers. In response, God was gracious and answered me. In true Biblical fashion, God was kind to me and gave me truth infused with grace. He neither condemned me nor overwhelmed me with too much information. This truth that I have learned has already begun to change my relationships, as well as my prayer life.

Our life is made up of a series of moments in which we can respond well or react poorly. God is gracious and He can certainly redirect us. However, for every positive interaction we have, this creates more positive feelings, as well as the determination to try again when things go wrong. This goes for our prayer life as well as our interactions with others. When we practice honesty and grace, the results begin to change our reality and day-to-day experiences.

Name one thing that is weighing you down and discuss it with your spouse using the non-verbal communication technique.

EVALUATE YOUR PROGRESS

1. What did you learn about your spouse?

2. What did you learn about your own emotions and perspective?

3. Are you motivated to do this again with another topic?

DIGGING DEEPER INTO CHAPTER 3

The Word search for this chapter is
precious

Psalms 139:17-18

Isaiah 43:4

Proverbs 3:15

Proverbs 31:10

CHAPTER 4

REMEMBER AND ACKNOWLEDGE YOUR PAST

Honestly, I [Matt] initially struggled with the concept of how much influence I should let the past have on me. *If I decide to look back, am I somehow not putting my faith in the Lord? Did I even have enough memories to make a difference?* There are several verses in the Bible that specifically warn us not to look back, even to the point that it says we are not fit for the Kingdom if we do (see Luke 9:62). If that's what the Bible intended, then I had a problem. *Was I wrong to look back?*

I don't believe so, for in doing that, the Lord has brought understanding, healing, and restoration in my relationship with my wife and with Him. This sets up an interesting tension. As Christians we believe that the Bible does not contradict itself. The Word of the Lord is truth and the standard of faith to which we aspire. It would seem, however, that there is a contradiction here—to look back or not.

I have good news. The whole Bible is a look back at our collective past. Applying the truth of our past helps our perspective of the present become more clear. The Bible calls us to remember about 250 times. That is a significant number of times and dwarfs the times we are told not to look back. He wants us to remember what He has done in the past as stated in Deuteronomy 6:12, and 8:2. Paul wrote we are to remember and maintain our traditions in 1 Corinthians 11:2. We are to remember the teachings of Jesus as stated in Acts 20:35. Revelation 2:5 says we are to remember from where we have fallen so we can repent.

We investigate our past when we reminisce about fun or positive memories. We may feel a rush of warm, fuzzy feelings as a result. Looking back also involves considering some things we perhaps would rather not address. We can accept that looking at the positive memories impacts us, but then the negative ones need to be suppressed or ignored? As much as we would like to think or wish that our past does not influence us, it does. We can try to avoid it, but that will only make things worse.

We are reminded of our children during the season of potty training. We would often ask them, knowing full well the answer, "Did you poop?" They would stand there, and with a serious, straight face, say no. This was neither the truth, nor did it alter the need to change the dirty diaper. Looking back at our past may feel a lot like that dirty diaper. We don't particularly want to acknowledge that the nasty stuff is there. However, if we don't address it, we will get a spiritual or emotional rash! If we are the parent in the relationship, we can more easily see what will happen. But how many of us enjoy cleaning up the mess? That rash is an irritation. Not addressing our emotions can also cause us to be irritated and easily triggered and we don't really understand the reason why.

It's interesting that positive memories emerge, stay in our mind for a time, and leave after we have engaged them. They generate positive healthy emotions. Negative memories will arrive, and they tend to stay for a long time and often repeatedly return because we don't engage them like we do the positive ones. This causes guilt and shame, which causes us to try and avoid the messy diaper instead of dealing with the problem.

While guilt can be motivating, shame is a more permanent state, causing us to feel that they are somehow flawed or evil, and that nothing will ever change. Although it's more difficult to accomplish, addressing the negative will have the same impact as addressing the positive if we deal with them honestly and directly. Looking back through the lens of Scripture builds on the idea that our array of emotions impacts our reactions—sometimes subconsciously.

Having a conversation with ourselves and the Lord becomes much easier and more understandable when we bring our history into the light of conscious day. We engage our past for understanding and forgiveness. The words of Scripture were given to primarily show us our sin, our need for Jesus, and God's plan for redemption. There are also principles that show us our need to become more like Jesus. The biblical word for that is *sanctification*. Engaging our emotions opens our desire and ability to apply what the Scriptures teach.

John 1:5 states, "The light shines in the darkness, and the darkness has not overcome it." Milan Yerkovich calls this confrontation of our past a journey of emotional sanctification. Once we have a more accurate and complete picture of our emotions, we are better able to address and change them. Exodus 20:5 states, "You shall not bow down to them or serve them, for I the Lord your God am a jealous God, visiting the iniquity of the fathers on the children to the third and the fourth generation of those who hate me." We can break that cycle in our own generation once and for all, thus not passing those problems and tendencies on to our kids and future generations.

When we look at our past to redeem it and not live by it, we then realize that God is doing something new when we remember. He wants to set us free. We often look back to rehearse or to blame, but God wants us to look back because we have a role to play if we are to experience our sanctification. Philippians 3:13-14 (AMP) says, "for the prize of the upward call of God in Christ Jesus."

Let's go back to my [Matt's] journey. I thought I had a pretty good handle on who I was as a person. It was not until I went back to the past that I was able to get to the future by understanding that my avoiding interactions was not how God made me—it's how I had allowed myself to become. I would never have guessed that flipping through the Sears Christmas catalog would have such an impact. Most of the catalog was fun. Dreaming of the next Legos or Star Wars action toys even as an adult is still enjoyable. Unfortunately, the other part of the catalog included the bra and underwear section, tame by today's standards. However, what those sections did was spark an interest that would lead to a profound impact on how I saw myself and how I interacted with others.

The Sears catalog combined with watching shows on television that showed the girls being interested in the guys had a significant negative influence on who I saw in myself. When I did not experience those interactions in my real life, then I turned inward, believing that I was not being pursued in that way because I was not worthy. I found out later that those shows depicted a false narrative. After sharing this publicly, I also found out I was not alone in the impact that catalog experience had in the journey of others.

Now that I have a better understanding of what contributed to my personality, emotions, and faith, the goal is to dig deeper so I can overcome that pattern and learn how to more effectively speak with others. How do we unlock our past in a way that helps us effectively understand it and share it with others? We do that by speaking to be known and listening to understand. The Lord can give us great insight through conversations with others, which we will explore more in the next few chapters.

MARRIAGE MATTERS TOOLS FOR CHAPTER 4

Our journey to understand our present by looking at our past requires some preparation. We started sharing what that looked like for Matt in this chapter. Now, it is your turn.

1. Start by taking some time to think about and reflect on your past.

2. Read Psalm 139:23. Pray that the Lord will search your heart and give you some memories to unpack. These most often will be experiences where your needs were not met, and that is having an impact today. Remember that our parents/caregivers also had wounds, so our look back is not to judge them. In fact, our new perspective will eventually help us to look with more compassion towards them and ourselves. You may not initially have memories that come to mind. That is okay. Keep searching through prayer and conversations with others.

    Again, use the non-verbal communication technique. If going to your spouse would cause some conflict, then seek out a trusted friend, for our friends can often see things that we cannot.

3. Record what you find in a journal. It will be important for us to have this as we look back later for healing.

EVALUATE YOUR PROGRESS

1. What did you learn about your spouse?

2. What did you learn about your own emotions and perspective?

3. Are you motivated to do this again with another topic?

DIGGING DEEPER INTO CHAPTER 4

This chapter's Word search is
fear

Isaiah 41:10

Psalm 34:4

Proverbs 29:25

Philippians 4:6

SPEAK TO BE KNOWN AND UNDERSTOOD, NOT TO BLAME

Proverbs 15 has quite a bit to say about the words we speak and the power they have. Verse four is especially relevant to our conversation here: "The soothing tongue is a tree of life, but a perverse tongue crushes the spirit." *Crush* creates quite a word picture. The picture that comes to my mind is an eggshell. When it is crushed, it shatters into many little pieces. Something that once offered protection is then rendered completely useless.

Our words crush the spirit, our own and that of others, in various ways. Some run away and avoid any conflict or confrontation. Others may try harder to soothe the speaker by offering something positive that will distract them from the issue at hand. Responding aggressively or even violently towards the speaker can also be an indication of a crushed soul. Someone who has spent most of their life as a victim will understandably just take it and not respond. They will stay in the proximity of the speaker but will roll themselves out as a doormat and allow the speaker to step all over them.

Another group who are crushed will do everything to cover up the fact that they are indeed crushed. They will attempt to control their circumstances and the people around them so they do not have to reveal or acknowledge their own pain. Each reaction is evidence that pain is present. That's the reason understanding emotions is important in healing and growing in sanctification.

Engaging our emotions lowers the temperature of a discussion and gets to the heart of the issue in a way that a factual discussion does not. The irony of avoiding emotions in favor of facts is that our emotions are factual. Understanding ours helps us understand the emotions of the person with whom we are engaging as well. In secular circles, this is called emotional intelligence, which starts with self-awareness and then leads to the awareness of what others are feeling.

Scripture is impressive in how much it teaches us in a practical way about relationships and communication. Ellen and I found a fun way to find out a lot of information in a quick period and that is to machine gun questions and answers. We run through a long list of questions and answer them quickly with a sentence or two. We then can go back if we say something or hear something that piques our interest so we can explore it further. We will state the verse and then quickly state how it ties into marriage, one after the other.

1. Let's start with 1 John 1:9 – "If we confess our sins, He is faithful and just to forgive us our sins and to cleanse us from all unrighteousness." Confessing is an important consideration in speaking honestly because it keeps the focus of the conversation on the speaker, not pointing the finger of blame at our spouse.

2. Ephesians 5:21 – "Submit to one another out of reverence for Christ." Humbly communicating a felt need will deepen the intimacy of any relationship. Submission is important in the role of the speaker and the listener. When both are submissive, the

effectiveness of the communication increases. We set aside our agenda and need to be heard for now and really listen.

3. First Peter 2:18 (BSB) – "Servants, submit yourselves to your masters with all respect, not only to those who are good and gentle, but even to those who are unreasonable." We have all been hurt in relationships. When that pain is from a current relationship, we are to submit and support our partner, even when our spouse is triggered and going off emotionally.

Please know that we are not talking about any type of abuse here. If abuse is present, the first step is to get to safety. Being submissive is not allowing oneself to be a doormat. It takes great strength to submit ourselves to someone else, especially when we are in the heat of a moment. Listening to someone who is in authority over us is not always easy. We get that. But having to do so when they are unreasonable and not gentle and disrespectful? That seems unfair, but that is the biblical standard. We are submitting to each other when we keep the focus on ourselves when speaking instead of blasting away at our partner.

4. First John 3:1 – "See what kind of love the Father has given to us, that we should be called children of God; and so we are. The reason why the world does not know us is that it did not know Him. Beloved, we are God's children now, and what we will be has not yet appeared; but we know that when He appears we shall be like him, because we shall see Him as He is." *It is important that we see our spouse as they are and not how we want them to be.* Ellen and I wanted the other to be more like ourselves. Ellen wanted Matt to be more in touch with his emotions. Matt wanted Ellen not to be controlled as much by hers. Our intentions were good, but we didn't really see or hear each other until we spoke with and not at each other, as the Bible directed us to do.

The timing of our speech is also important. Saying the right thing at the wrong time can be as damaging as saying the wrong thing at any time. We help ourselves and others when we guard our lips. Proverbs 13:3 finishes that thought by saying we preserve their lives, but those who speak rashly will come to ruin. When we speak and feel the need to vent or "word vomit" all over anyone who will listen, we might feel better for a while after we're done. However, just like with an addiction, the good feeling quickly vanishes, and we may or may not realize we have done more harm than good, as the Lord warned us would happen.

Positively or negatively, what we have in our hearts influences whether we react or respond. Jesus said in Luke 16:4, "A good man brings good things out of the good stored up in his heart, and an evil man brings evil things out of the evil stored up in his heart. For the mouth speaks what the heart is full of." Notice the source is the same whether the man is good or evil. To apply that truth to relationships, our reactions and responses reflect what is in our hearts.

Understanding what is there and how it got there can greatly impact whether we add to the pain or work to bring comfort and healing. If we don't understand that reality when we speak, we may unknowingly do more damage than we intended or thought possible. When we understand the power of effective listening, then we can intentionally bring long-term positive change with our words instead of our judgment.

The last two Scriptures we will consider about this topic for now are found in the New Testament. Ephesians 4:29 says, "Do not let any unwholesome talk come out of your mouths, but only what is helpful for building others up according to their needs, that it may benefit those who listen." A few things stand out in this verse. We know and can learn our spouse's needs through wholesome honest conversation. Unwholesome speech is an indication that something unhealthy and problematic is going on. When our spouse blows up at us, we need to acknowledge the depth and intensity of their pain. The bigger the blow up, the deeper the pain. Proverbs tells us we are foolish if we rely on our own opinion rather than pursuing understanding. The negative patterns we have developed are foolish. Although we may feel better initially, those patterns never lead to a positive step in the right direction.

And then Paul wrote in Colossians 4:5-6, "Be wise in the way you act toward outsiders; make the most of every opportunity. Let your conversation be always full of grace, seasoned with salt, so that you may know how to answer everyone." Our most important "outsider" is our spouse. Other verses use the concept of neighbor to describe the person or people to which we are speaking. We often speak to others with more love, compassion, and respect than we do to our spouse. The Bible calls us to speak with grace and truth first and foremost to our spouse. Notice that grace is first on the list, and for good reason.

Let's go back and pick up my [Matt's] experience with the Sears Christmas catalog. I was asked to speak to a group of men about pornography. I was ready to go with presenting some material that I had learned in a TED talk called "The Great Porn Experiment." The talk included some good factual research about pornography, much of which would have already been heard by most in the audience. However, the Lord had other plans. He used this preparation time to uncover something significant in understanding my comfort with being alone versus being social and getting to know others.

There were two main points to that talk. This wasn't just quote-a-Scripture-and-do-it moment. Our past will impact our present and future. Speaking to others showed me that although I never did struggle with a porn addiction, how I viewed myself and others was impacted considerably. I shared the story to be known. Others knowing my story and being encouraged as a result helped me grow in a way that blaming my past, others, or circumstances never could. Not that we want others to struggle, but it is good to know that we are not alone.

The abbreviated version of the story is that the girls I knew were not reacting to me in the way I saw portrayed in the media. The catalog pictures were framed to elicit emotions which would hopefully lead to a purchase. For me, the pictures were attractive, made me feel good and therefore sparked a desire to have a relationship with a person like the ones pictured. I then saw the behavior of how the girls my age and a little older were portrayed on the TV and movies as normal, but it was not. On television or in the movies, the guy ended up in a relationship with the girl, and that wasn't happening for me. So I concluded I must not be someone who was interesting enough to have the girl want a relationship with me. If the girls were not interested, then why would the guys be either? (I was only interested in a romantic relationship with the girls.)

Rather than being the fun, interesting guy I was created to

be, I was reserved. I was involved in activities, but I didn't take advantage of the opportunity that those activities provided to engage personally with others. I interpreted it that others must not find me interesting since they were not responding as I thought they "should." In truth, I didn't give others a chance because I was not interested in proactively learning the skills I needed in those situations. Being reclusive was much easier.

Surprisingly, marriage didn't change that faulty view I had of myself. I knew that my wife saw me and found me valuable. That still did not translate into any change in my interaction with others. The Lord would have to put me in a public speaking platform for that to occur, one where I was not only facilitating a class, but doing so with material and a curriculum I had created. That represented quite a change for someone who had believed for decades that I wasn't interesting enough to influence others.

There was a benefit to my struggle. I believe God used it to stop me from being in relationships growing up that I was not ready to handle. I see His work in that and I'm thankful for it. However, that same approach is not now effective for adult relationships. That includes being romantic with my wife or non-romantic interactions with others.

We often focus on our relational challenges and how ineffective listening contributes to poor communication. However, ineffective speaking causes just as many issues. Proverbs 16:24 states, "Gracious words are a honeycomb, sweet to the soul and healing to the bones." We can relate to the first part of the verse about being sweet. The end of the verse is what stands out the most. We don't necessarily believe that our words contribute to our or anyone's physical healing.

However, there is a large body of research emerging in this area. Dr. Curt Thompson's *Anatomy of the Soul* gives a more detailed treatment of that subject. I [Matt] would recommend picking up one of his books. However, God stated this truth long ago in Proverbs. In many ways, the speaking side of our discussion is easier than listening. Both are needed, so let's take a closer look at the power of listening.

MARRIAGE MATTERS TOOLS FOR CHAPTER 5

We all have areas with which we struggle, and the intensity of the struggle can vary. Take a moment to honestly evaluate your skills as a speaker.

When I speak to my spouse do I do the following?

1. Understand the barriers to speaking which I struggle with most.

2. Stick to one topic.

3. Avoid blaming others and circumstances.

4. Defend my point of view as right.

5. Interrupt when others are speaking.

6. Do I trust my spouse's motives?

Keep in mind that there are no right or wrong answers to these questions. It is important for growth to have an honest evaluation of where you are. Before ending this time, pray and ask the Lord for His insights.

EVALUATE YOUR PROGRESS

1. What did you learn about your skills?

2. What did you learn about your own emotions and perspective?

3. Are you motivated to do this again with another topic?

DIGGING DEEPER INTO CHAPTER 5

This chapter's Word search is
harsh words

Proverbs 12:18

James 1:26

James 3:5-7

Proverbs 13:3

CHAPTER 6

LISTEN TO UNDERSTAND, NOT TO CHANGE OR CRITIQUE

The word *listen* appears almost 300 times in the Bible. One of those times is in Luke 8:18 where Jesus said, "Therefore consider carefully how you listen. Whoever has will be given more; whoever does not have, even what they think they have will be taken from them." If we listen well, our relationship will grow. If we don't, we won't even realize what we are missing or that we don't have the depth of relationship we thought we had.

Romans 12:2 states, "Do not conform to the pattern of this world, but be transformed by the renewing of your mind. Then you will be able to test and approve what God's will is—his good, pleasing and perfect will." Testing and discerning are not easy. Whether it is with the Lord or a human relationship, we won't find what is good, acceptable, or perfect without listening. This reality applies to any type of relationship, including the most important ones we have with the Father and then with our spouse.

It sounds trite but if we take the time and walk in someone else's shoes so we can truly understand them (not necessarily agree with them), we will discover our differences are not all that different. Listening affords us the opportunity to do just that. It is so important that we spend time in community and in conversation, sharing openly and honestly with one person those things that affect and hurt us. For listening to be effective, we need to dig deeper than just facts. We need to understand the emotions that drive the perspective and the words and deeds. It is easy in our culture to become isolated and feel alone. In this generation, there are more incidences of depression and anxiety than ever before.

In a world of social media, we are inundated everyday with other people's "perfect" lives, thoughts, and dinner plates and dates. There is tremendous pressure to look right and think right. We compare ourselves to others, knowing our own junk, and therefore feeling shame and inadequate when compared to the lives portrayed on social media. Why doesn't 24-hour access cause us to feel included, loved, wanted, or seen and heard? We are a keyboard away from millions yet too many feel isolated and alone.

It's because none of that relates to real life and relationships. Social media provides a powerful tool, but we must acknowledge its limitations. Information is available online but rich interactive dialogue and encouragement are best saved for face-to-face intimate relationships. Sharing our deeper personal challenges is better done privately in the presence of those who love us and whom we trust.

We share some of our "stuff" there and in this book to encourage and teach you. We have spent years going through a process of healing. That process should neither be broadcast while it is happening nor after without the consent of both parties. Social media should be used as a tool to encourage conversation. When most of it is negative, it is understandable why so many react to it and avoid it.

We learn about others through listening face-to-face or through reading. What are our barriers to listening and understanding in those situations?

1. We have our own agendas we want to promote.

2. We have our own past pain which easily triggers our need to react or defend.

3. We don't really understand our history and the impact it has on what drives our thoughts, actions, emotions, and reactions.

4. We hear corroborating "evidence" in our culture and conversations with like-minded people which hardens our personal perspective as "right."

5. We make assumptions of others that influence and limit our engagement with them and contribute to the divide.

6. We are afraid of what we are hearing or what we assume we will be hearing later in the conversation.

7. Are we too busy or do we make excuses? But in reality, dialogue and communication take time.

8. We forget that an outburst of negative emotions is not irrational, but can be understandable as a reasonable if intense expression of pain.

Those barriers and a few others contribute to creating a pattern of ineffective listening. We need some sort of accountability when we allow the barriers we create to block or hinder relationship. Without that, we will develop and sustain habits that lead to ineffective listening. Effective listening is an important skill whether we are sharing with our spouse, our friends, or a trained professional therapist. Listening helps to create community and fosters an understanding that we are not as alone or unique as we previously thought.

Ellen and I would repeatedly have the same conversations in the same way. Our ineffective listening led to a flawed strategy that if we just said the same thing one more time, everything would improve, and the other person would finally "understand." One such discussion went on for a few years, centering on our jobs and the limited financial resources we had at the time. Friends of ours had started working as house parents. I thought that sounded like a fantastic idea: ten days on, four off. One of Ellen's concerns was the limited amount of time we were already not spending together. If we accepted this job, we would get to spend a lot more time together. Sounded like a good solution for her concerns to me. That meant I was listening to her, right?

What's more, this job would have helped financially because housing and food were paid for. That job would have reduced my stress level as well as met Ellen's needs. To my surprise, Ellen was not on board the 50 or more times I brought up the subject. I tried all kinds of angles for months to persuade her to see things my way. Although the job solution seemed to cover our most frequent stressors, my persistent pursuit of trying to convince her showed I was not listening. My own personal desires were getting in the way causing barriers to communication. Biblical principles of listening helped us break down those barriers. Here are a few we have found.

1. James 1:19: – *"My dear brothers and sisters, take note of this: Everyone should be quick to listen, slow to speak and slow to become angry."* You must set aside your agenda for communication to occur. Otherwise, when your agenda isn't being accomplished, frustration sets in and distracts you from really hearing what the other is saying. Frustration and anger were a big part of our discussions during that season. I [Matt] was fast to speak and slow to listen. I did not recognize the anger I had before it came in full view. You can and must take those angry thoughts captive. Setting them aside temporarily to listen improves your ability to hear and understand. For years, I did neither.

2. Psalm 116:1-4 – *"I love the LORD, for He heard my voice; He heard my cry for mercy. Because He turned his ear to me, I will call on him as long as I live. The cords of death entangled me, the anguish of the grave came over me; I was overcome by distress and sorrow. Then I called on the name of the LORD: 'LORD, save me!'"* Verse two is interesting. We are to "turn our ears" if we want to hear and understand. For years, decades even, if I [Matt] am honest, I thought it was fine for me to listen while doing another task. There surely are times when multitasking is appropriate. However, to effectively listen, Scripture says we need to be physically focused on our spouse. We must "turn our ear." The dishes can wait for another hour or two.

Then look at the power of effective listening mentioned in

verse four. The more we listen in love, the more people are willing to share. Listening helps others be more willing to reach out. Our skills as a listener can help move someone from crippling despair to hope. Matt thought he was listening about the job, but he was entangled by only listening to the parts he wanted to hear. Listening in part, like obeying in part, is not really listening.

3. Matthew 7:24 – *"Therefore everyone who hears these words of mine and puts them into practice is like a wise man who built his house on the rock."* Ultimately, a change in behavior starts with a change in thought. Or does it? The analogy of which came first, the chicken or the egg, comes to mind. Is it our actions that we put into practice that helps to heal our despair or is it a change in emotions that motivates the change in behavior? Both are correct. The benefits of listening jump off the page in Scripture. Listening helps us to be wise and puts us on a firm foundation of rock. We both needed to make a wise decision about this possible job because if we accepted it, our lives would be completely changed.

4. Philippians 4:9 – *"Whatever you have learned or received or heard from me, or seen in me, put it into practice. And the God of peace will be with you."* The next step in our emotional journey after obedience is listening which brings peace. Listening is not a one-and-done event but takes practice. I [Matt] was a clarinet player as a child. My parents will attest to this after enduring years of insisting I practice and the many discussions around my lack in that area. It would have been much easier, I thought, if learning how to play effectively only took one session of practice. The truth is, each session of practice built on the previous, even if there was not a noticeable change. Over the course of time, persistent practice made a difference. Not practicing intentionally also made a difference. I came back to school after not playing over the summer and my skills were worse. The same applies to the skill of listening. Be intentional and persistent in listening.

5. Revelation 3:20 – *"Here I am! I stand at the door and knock. If anyone hears my voice and opens the door, I will come in and eat with that person, and they with me."* Listening encourages fellowship—with God and others. Think about that person or groups of people you enjoy being with as adults. They listen to you and you to them. Not too many of us would go back out to dinner with someone who ignored us even when discussing surface topics like opinions and hobbies.

We decided to spend some time with the friends who were in the job I [Matt] wanted. We asked a lot of questions and got to see the house live and in action. I was not-so-secretly hoping that the experience would change Ellen's mind. It did not. Why? Because I had not listened to Ellen and arranged the meeting anyway. I kept pushing, hoping that I would get her to agree to my perspective.

6. Malachi 2:2 – *"If you do not listen, and if you do not resolve to honor my name," says the Lord Almighty, "I will send a curse on you, and I will curse your blessings. Yes, I have already cursed them, because you have not resolved to honor me."* Listening honors the other person and avoids a curse and other bad things that could happen. This one jumps right off the page as I think about how much struggle and pain were caused by my lack of listening. Ultimately, after a long pursuit of trying to persuade Ellen, I listened to her concerns. It was interesting that her concerns were the same as the ones I was suppressing in my own mind. We decided not to pursue the job, and I believe that we avoided some challenges that would not have been in the best interests of our family.

7. Proverbs 4:20-21 – *"My son, pay attention to what I say; turn your ear to my words. Do not let them out of your sight, keep them within your heart."* Paying attention when we listen enables us to keep what we learned accessible. We have a saying in our home, "If you snooze, you lose." This most often applies to leftover pizza, but the principle is still the same in listening.

Focusing on listening addresses what others are experiencing and trying to tell us through their words. We can reduce the stress patterns we develop over time simply by listening. When we listen, we notice those "here we go again" discussions that lead to a divide in our ability to engage. Someone who feels heard is not as likely to feel the need to repeat the discussion. That does not mean that past feelings won't arise in new circumstances, but we found we do not have the conversations about the same circumstance again when we improve our ability to listen with the intent to understand.

8. Galatians 3:5 – *"So again I ask, does God give you his Spirit and work miracles among you by the works of the law, or by believing what you heard?"* Listening gives God a vehicle through which He can send His Spirit to do His transformational work. He works miracles when we listen. That is good news. We often want to jump in and fix something. We don't need eloquent responses to help in healing, a bold move indeed when the Bible says the opposite. Our job is to listen; it is the Lord's job to bring healing.

Effective speaking causes others to be open to listen from our example. Our transparency inspires our spouse to become more transparent which then inspires us even more. If you want to change a downward or stagnant pattern with your spouse, then listen to understand. You can overcome many barriers by listening and being obedient to the Scriptures. Emotional healing is possible but takes time. Listen in such a way that leads to healing. They lead us to the last and most important principle, which is speaking and listening lead to understanding and bonding.

MARRIAGE MATTERS TOOLS FOR CHAPTER 6

Take time to evaluate your skills as a listener. Are you really listening? Be honest. In this last section, did you gloss over or skim the Bible verses? I know that I [Matt]do that, seeking to get an overall picture of what was going on, but missing the details. The details of our emotions are often more important to understand than the facts and circumstances of the situation. As a listener, are you asking clarifying questions to understand more deeply? We assume that we know what is going on and do not bother to check the details. Capturing the details using reflection will deepen your understanding.

When I listen to my spouse do I do the following?

1. Understand the barriers to listening which I struggle with most.
2. Criticize the speaker.
3. Seek to end the conversation early.
4. Become defensive.
5. Interrupt when others are speaking.
6. Distrust my spouse's motive.

Keep in mind that there are no right or wrong answers to these questions. It is important for growth to have an honest evaluation where you are currently. Before ending this time, pray and ask the Lord for His insights.

EVALUATE YOUR PROGRESS

1. What did you learn about your spouse?

2. What did you learn about your own emotions and perspective

3. Are you motivated to do this again with another topic?

DIGGING DEEPER INTO CHAPTER 6

Read the following and ask the Lord how this applies to your effectiveness as a listener

Jeremiah 33:3

Jeremiah 29:12

CHAPTER 7

UNDERSTANDING AND BONDING – MAKING THE ORDINARY EXTRAORDINARY

Our first Christmas, we were so excited to share our gifts with one another that we started a lasting Christmas Eve tradition. I [Ellen] remember at least one of those things that I bought today. Neither of us had come from an open-one-present-on Christmas-Eve background. However, as I wrote that, I was reminded how this was not totally true. Growing up, I spied a present that had a very distinctive shape to it, one that my brother had purchased for me. I knew it was the thing that I had desired, perhaps more than any other gift that year. I continually pestered my parents to allow us to open just one present on Christmas Eve. Being the baby of the family, I got my way. Forty-plus years later, I remember that the flying Nerf robot did not disappoint! But also, from that time on, we started our own family tradition of opening one present on Christmas Eve.

We came into our first Christmas as a married couple discussing this very thing. We agreed we might be able to open one Christmas present on Christmas Eve, but it would have to stop there. Or would it? Over the course of the evening, we quickly decided to do more, and proceeded to open all but one. We stopped only because we wanted to have something to look forward to the following day. We have done the same ever since. When our kids came along, it was a lot of late nights, and present wrapping, and cleaning up, and making magic before we could enjoy our tradition. Some years, we considered ourselves lucky to be wrapped up and ready by 1:30 a.m. I think we might have had a 3:00 a.m. end time one year.

Our tradition held, though, through all the kid years. We would finally be alone and would turn off all the lights, except for the Christmas tree. We used to have eggnog every year, but we have made some concessions when it comes to old age and diabetes. We might play music or we might not, but we will spend some time talking and praying together before we get to the presents. It goes by so quickly! We still have the tradition of leaving one present for each other for morning that we can then open with our kids—just one.

You probably have events like this too, things that you look forward to once a year or less as you anticipate a family vacation, which may not happen every year. (We are still hoping to go back to build on our 25-year-anniversary Tennessee trip.) These bonding experiences are great moments in a relationship. However, they are not sufficient by virtue of their sparsity to hold us together. Several years ago, we recognized the bonding that happens, not only in those great mountain-top experiences, but also in the ordinary and every day. The word *extraordinary* is made up of two words, *extra* and *ordinary*. We began to see the value of driving to pick up a kid from band practice or folding laundry together. It is in these ordinary moments that we find the glue of our relationship because we can make the ordinary extraordinary.

I [Matt] often expect my wife to see things my way and when I ask her for something, I expect it to be done. However, when the reverse happens, it is not the same story. She asked me to spray down the shower while she was working and I was off. First, the bathroom is her job. I had other plans that were equally and maybe more important. *She can do it after work* or so I thought. It only took several hours of me trying to rationalize not doing it before something changed.

I think the Lord's patience with me on this issue had run out when He asked, "Matt, how would you respond if your wife ignored something you asked her to do?" I went and sprayed out the shower. Her asking should be enough. How foolish was I for wasting far more time building my case to get out of it than the time it took just to do the task?

Our relationship will be far better when our spouse feels heard and appreciated. We have a choice. How we react or respond to our spouses over time creates a pattern of interaction. Those patterns can either take away from or contribute to our understanding of our spouse. Let's look at what the Bible says about understanding and bonding.

1. Ecclesiastes 4:9-12 – *"Two are better than one, because they have a good return for their labor: If either of them falls down, one can help the other up. But pity anyone who falls and has no one to help them up. Also, if two lie down together, they will keep warm. But how can one keep warm alone? Though one may be overpowered, two can defend themselves. A cord of three strands is not quickly broken."*
    What the Lord describes in those verses is the bonding we see in healing. The strength of the three-fold cord is stronger than just the strands by themselves.

    This is also one of the reasons that the Lord created the primary human relationship model in the Garden. The physical warmth we provide for each other is something we can't do alone, even if we have a strong relationship with Jesus. Relationship skills we learned in our past contribute to or take away from the strength of that cord. The Lord could provide all of that need for strength directly and does that for some people. For those of us who are married, He has given us our spouses to strengthen that bond with Him for both us and our spouse—two for the price of one. Acknowledge that your spouse is a gift, receive them from Him, and they will bring you comfort, warmth, and strength.

2. Psalm 139:1 (ESV) – *"O Lord, you have searched me and known me! You know when I sit."* Our spouses are our most intimate relationship apart from the Lord. We joke about how we already know what our spouse is thinking or that we can finish their sentences accurately before they do. In all seriousness, we can know how our spouse will respond or react. In fact, we should know our spouses well enough that we can often finish their sentences. That can be a trap as well, however, because we don't want our own assumptions to prevent us from effectively listening. Some of the knowledge we have about our partner comes from experience. Some of it could be assumptions we have not confirmed with them.

   Our spouses are an earthly representation and fulfillment of this verse. We are imperfect so we need to help fill in by expressing our needs honestly and fully. The Lord is perfect and does not need our help to know or understand, yet He still requires us to tell Him for our benefit—so we can be clear. Searching through a relationship with our spouse and in prayer time with the Lord are both effective techniques for attaining the understanding we seek for healing and comfort.

3. Galatians 6:1-2 – *"Brothers and sisters, if someone is caught in a sin, you who live by the Spirit should restore that person gently. But watch yourselves, or you also may be tempted. Carry each other's burdens, and in this way you will fulfill the law of Christ."* These verses provide a practical application for how to achieve understanding. The better the understanding, the deeper the bond. There are several important points of application here. Gentleness is much more than just a calm, soothing voice. Being gentle at its essence is listening to understand, not to correct or respond to persuade. We are to bear with the other, exhibiting

empathy for their feelings. Try to grasp their perspective through the eyes of the other person. Go deeper than just the facts and thoughts. True empathy involves understanding how the other person really feels.

4. Psalm 119:130 – *"The unfolding of your words gives light; it gives understanding to the simple,"* and *Proverbs 3:13: "Blessed are those who find wisdom, those who gain understanding."* The principles of these two verses considered together are an important turning point in moving from speaking and talking to understanding and bonding. How we speak shines light on the truth and is a blessing to those who are involved. Understanding leads to bonding as we empathize with what the other is going through.

How does Scripture define bonding and understanding in marriage? Let's go back to our machine gun approach. Colossians 3:12-15:

Therefore, as God's chosen people, holy and dearly loved, clothe yourselves with compassion, kindness, humility, gentleness and patience. Bear with each other and forgive one another if any of you has a grievance against someone. Forgive as the Lord forgave you. And over all these virtues put on love, which binds them all together in perfect unity. Let the peace of Christ rule in your hearts, since as members of one body you were called to peace. And be thankful. Finally, brothers and sisters, rejoice! Strive for full restoration, encourage one another, be of one mind, live in peace. And the God of love and peace will be with you.

How we frame our words is just as important, perhaps more so than the actual words we use. Consider Ephesians 4:2-3: "Be completely humble and gentle; be patient, bearing with one another in love. Make every effort to keep the unity of the Spirit through the bond of peace." Scripture states that our goals are unity and bonding. The easiest way to get there is taking the time to understand and developing the skills needed to do so. First Peter 3:8 further states, "Finally, all of you, be like-minded, be sympathetic, love one another, be compassionate and humble."

Unity in marriage does not mean that we are both the same: think alike, act like, etc. Whether we are talking about a group of believers or an individual marriage, our bonds are made stronger because we are different. If we were all the same, there would be no one to challenge us to grow. God made each of us individually, then brought us together for a purpose. We grow to be more united when we engage our differences. They push us to understand more deeply.

Our differences also provide us with an opportunity to deal with conflict. The Lord's love for us is unconditional. Making things right during and after a conflict gives us an opportunity to practice the virtues listed in Colossians 3:14: "And over all these virtues put on love, which *binds* them all together in perfect unity." The context of this verse is important for understanding how this verse applies. Earlier in verse 11, the writer stated, "Where there is neither Greek nor Jew, circumcision nor uncircumcision, barbarian, Scythian, bond nor free: but Christ is all, and in all."

We are united in physical and spiritual intimacy, both being important commands from the Lord. Although it would be a mistake to insist on intimacy because the Bible says so, intimacy on multiple levels keeps us bonded together as one. First Corinthians 7:1-4 says,

> Now concerning the matters about which you wrote: "It is good for a man not to have sexual relations with a woman." But because of the temptation to sexual immorality, each man should have his own wife and each woman her own husband. The husband should give to his wife her conjugal rights, and likewise the wife to her husband. For the wife does not have authority over her own body, but the husband does. Likewise the husband does not have authority over his own body, but the wife does. Do not deprive one another, except perhaps by agreement for a limited time, that you may devote yourselves to prayer; but then come together again, so that Satan may not tempt you because of your lack of self-control.

Notice the concept of authority in that passage, which doesn't mean to lord it over someone else. Intimacy exists when both parties sacrificially surrender themselves to the other. The Golden Rule, simply stated, is that we should do unto others as we would have them do unto us as stated in Luke 6:31. Unity is achievable when we hold ourselves to the same standard as we do our spouse.

This next part of our testimony in some ways makes me laugh. When we were first married, I [Matt] was finally in a position where we had a little extra money to spend. Well, it is a little closer because I had a credit card that had probably a little more available credit than I should have been allowed to have. I decided that it was important for me to have a new game system. I had previously had an Atari, which was fun, but Nintendo had cool graphics and I wanted to play the Nintendo. So I went out and purchased it for $300.00.

I brought it home and of course Ellen noticed. She decided that she wanted to have someone professionally paint a grapevine in our dining room, which cost us the same price as the video game system. So she called the painter and the work began. The painter did a masterful job. We were both pleased with the work. Pleased that is after I grumbled about the price. I grumbled, but we needed to keep things even. Ironically a few weeks later, I decided to return the game system because I got bored with it quickly. So we did return the Nintendo, but we could not return the painting. It is still a focal point in our dining room.

Jesus said in Mark 9:35, "Sitting down, Jesus called the Twelve and said, 'Anyone who wants to be first, must be the very last, and be servant of all.'" Bonding and understanding are achieved when we put the needs of our spouse ahead of our own. We will talk in a later chapter about how what we do can work against what we want. Paul touched on this concept in Romans 7:15-19.

> I do not understand what I do. For what I want to do I do not do, but what I hate I do. And if I do what I do not want to do, I agree that the law is good. As it is, it is no longer I, myself who do it, but it is sin living in me. For I know that good itself does not dwell in me, that is, in my sinful nature. For I have the desire to do what is good, but I cannot carry it out. For I do not do the good I want to do, but the evil I do not want to do—this I keep on doing.

We had many middle-of-the-night opportunities to serve in our marriage with four kids, whether it was tending to a crying baby, almost falling asleep leaning against the wall while the other fed the young child, or a run for some medicine so the other could feel better. We perhaps were understandably a little cranky when first awakened. Although it would have been easier to stay seated or lying in bed, the opportunities to be a blessing were far more rewarding despite how irritating the initial push to move may have felt. At times, it seemed like those nights would never end. In truth they did and in a blink of an eye, they are now decades in the past. It is much sweeter to look back and be able to have examples of going to care for our spouse and the kids instead of missing those opportunities by going back to sleep.

Honest self-evaluation gives a clearer picture of our part in the relationship, good and not so good. Psalm 139:1-2 states, "You have searched for me, Lord, and you know me. You know when I sit and when I rise. You perceive my thoughts from afar." The goal is not judgment of self or spouse but understanding. Our thoughts impact our actions. When we know what those are and where they come from in advance, we are better prepared when they arrive. Seeing each one's part in our interactions reduces the tendency to point fingers and judge.

Joy is an important component of bonding as Paul wrote in Philippians 2:1-2:

> Therefore if you have any encouragement from being united with Christ, if any comfort from his love, if any common sharing in the Spirit, if any tenderness and compassion, then make my joy complete by being like-minded, having the same love, being one in spirit and purpose.

We will have more testimonials as to how we implemented bonding in our marriage later in the book. For now, we simply need to be aware of our tendencies when dealing with stress, expectations, and emotions. They all play an important part in first understanding ourselves so that we can better see and understand our spouse.

MARRIAGE MATTERS TOOLS FOR CHAPTER 7

Let's take the next step of learning to listen reflectively. This is the foundation of what helped us enrich our relationship. Once we started being more effective at listening reflectively to one another, we were able to better understand each other.

Reflective listening involves the listener repeating back what they are hearing to make sure they have an accurate understanding of what the speaker is communicating. This benefits both parties for sometimes the clarification also helps the speaker to better communicate the issue. The typical comment by the listener would be "what I hear you saying is . . ." The speaker then approves the listener's understanding or adds non-critical correction. "What I meant was . ."

Remember that it is important for each of you to alternate roles between speaker and listener. If you need to limit the amount of time each of you has in each role, that is fine. As you practice and gain more experience, you will be able to stay in your roles longer. It's okay to take notes but that isn't always possible. Taking notes helps you to remember the details and ask more effective questions always with a view toward gaining a better understanding.

Now that you have had some time to evaluate your own speaking and listening skills, it is time to find out what your spouse thinks. Share your evaluations of your listening and speaking skills with your spouse. Remember your purpose is to be known not to blame. If your spouse gets defensive, listen to them. Reflect on what you are hearing.

1. What I found I struggle with most in speaking is . . .
2. What I found I struggle with most in listening is . . .
3. What I found that I do well when speaking is . . .
4. What I found that I do well when listening is . . .
5. Ask each other, "What do you find is the biggest obstacle to growth in talking about our relationship?"

Resist the urge to argue or defend. Ask questions to find out more. It is important to remember that you may not have the time to finish both roles at one time. Have one conversation in your original roles before switching from speaker to listener or vice versa. Make time in the present or plan a time soon for both of you to each have a turn as speaker and listener. Effective communication involves knowing when each role is needed.

EVALUATE YOUR PROGRESS

1. What did you learn about your spouse?

2. What did you learn about your own emotions and perspective

3. Are you motivated to do this again with another topic?

DIGGING DEEPER INTO CHAPTER 7

This chapter's Word search is
acceptance

Proverbs 10:32

Romans 15:7

John 6:37

Romans 14:1-4

SECTION 2

STRESS, EXPECTATIONS, AND EMOTIONS

If there is one story outside of Scripture that has had the most impact in my [Matt's] life, it would be the *Star Wars'* franchise. My interest in the galaxy that is far, far away is mostly for entertainment and fun. George Lucas, its creator, and I even share a birthday. Unfortunately, we don't share a bank account. Playing with *Star Wars* action figures and adventures in the woods helped me move from being a young padawan to a Jedi Master. I still will make the "buzz" swirling sound of a lightsaber even when I pick up the cardboard center of wrapping paper at Christmas. I mean, who doesn't? That never gets old.

Darth Vader, Luke Skywalker, and Boba Fett were a big part of my play time growing up. As my favorite all-time villain, Darth Vader is fascinating and intimidating at the same time. I vividly remember the opening scene of *A New Hope* and hiding my eyes for a short period of time—not too long, though, because I still wanted to see the next move. I won't spoil the ending just in case you have not seen the movie but intend to watch it someday.

All *Star Wars* fans like me wanted to find out what could possibly have caused a man to become a ruthless killer. When we first met little Ani, he fell instantly in love with Padme and asked if she was an angel. His first heroic act was to help some strangers win replacement parts for their ship in a very dangerous race. To that point in his life, little Ani was a slave.

As one of the deleted scenes revealed, Anakin had some understandable issues with anger at that young age. He did not ever like being called a slave. That anger seems to be justifiable given the circumstances of his life. Eventually, Anakin is freed, grows up, and is a powerful and successful Jedi. He starts on his training, but he never really deals with the loss of his mother and the guilt that caused. Not addressing those significant wounds led to something horrific. Unfortunately, for most of his adult life, his actions were not heroic.

What he was missing in his life was learning how to acknowledge and deal appropriately with stress, and the emotions of losing so many he loved and the expectations of being who others were referring to as the "Chosen One." The Jedi taught their followers to let go of what they were afraid to lose. Another way of saying to let go would be to deflect the emotions of an attachment. Love and attachment, they claim, were a path ultimately to the dark side. Rather than embracing his feelings, Anakin was told to bury his feelings and hide his motives. Ultimately that minimizing resulted in extreme reactions with a need to control and the desire to never fail again.

That drive not to fail caused him to reach out in desperation to a person who embodied everything he had spent his life fighting against in Palpatine. Anakin chose to murder and control others in a failed attempt to save the life of ones he loved. He lost so much control that it was his actions that led to the death of the one he loved the most. His intentions were perhaps understandable, but the results of his actions were the exact opposite of what he intended.

We often do the same thing, but on a much lesser scale albeit in real life (not in a movie). We can lose ourselves by not properly addressing our emotions. We end up doing the things that cause the destruction we so desperately want to avoid. We then start down a path that we think we can control. Ultimately, Darth Vader said that he must obey his master. A point that was not actually true, but he allowed himself to believe. He went from wanting control to being completely controlled by another until the end.

His life started and ended as a slave to others. He became a slave to the emperor in the process of trying to protect those he loved. Like Anakin, we can lose everything we strive to achieve in our desperation. Anakin believed a lie that kept him in bondage for most of his adult life. It was the love of his son that brought him back to the light. It was his son Luke who sought out Anakin. It was Luke's example of sacrifice that motivated Anakin to change. Anakin thought it was too late, but Luke showed him it was not.

The same is true for us. Unlike Anakin, we have resources that can help us see the truth of how stress, expectations, and emotions impact our reactions. Anakin, like us, desperately sought love and relationship. Anakin is an extreme example, but we can nevertheless learn from his story. We can lose everything we strove to get, or we can learn a different way of coping with stress and emotional conflict. This next section will discuss all three of those important components in our adult relationships. Our purpose, of course, is not to stop the greatest villain in the history of film, but to deepen our intimacy with those we love the most.

CHAPTER 8

DEFINING STRESS

The two greatest challenges in marriage are how we manage stress
and the expectations we have of ourselves and our spouse. The
best way to handle stress and expectations is to understand our
emotions—how and why they operate and what we can expect
when they are healed and under the Lordship of Christ—through
a biblical lens. We engage them to find comfort and healing
through sharing with our spouse.

I [Matt] recently talked with someone who was struggling with anxiety. They were told by a Christian counselor that we as Christians should not have anxiety. Fascinating that the Scripture says do not be afraid more than 300 times. Why? The Scripture was written in a time of oral tradition. When a verse is repeated, just imagine it's God taking a big highlighter to emphasize at that moment what is important. God knew we would be anxious and so He asked us not to be afraid.

Those multiple references are not to prove that we shouldn't be anxious but to provide encouragement and a way to peace *when*, not *if*, we are. This journey involves a much deeper dive into Scripture than just understanding the truth and theology of each verse. Applying our emotional responses and reactions to the verse deepens our understanding and our experience of the specific verse or passage. Both are important. We found that when we stopped at understanding the verse, we too often did not mature in our faith or our relationship.

One of the words we use is *triggered* in describing our stress. Right now, at the time of this writing, I [Ellen] am feeling triggered. I am feeling scattered and unlovable, and I have the feeling that things will never change—at least not for the good. What is having me feel this way? Truthfully, I cannot say. I have examined those things that might be triggering me, but none of them seem to fit. A trigger, by the way, is defined as something that causes an emotional reaction, to the extent that our feelings don't match with our circumstances. Some may call that overreacting, but for the person triggered, it seems natural. The situation reminds us of something from our past which we might not even be able to put into words.

Even after learning to understand and acknowledge them, our strongest triggers can still happen, not as much as they used to, but they still happen. Oftentimes, my husband and I will find ourselves grocery shopping for our Friday night dates. My husband will often get his own cart, and while we are shopping together, he will just disappear. He doesn't answer his phone, so I must go find him.

A typical, perhaps even understandable, response might be some minor irritation. For me, this is not the case. As such, my brain goes straight to rage, which isn't normal. It took me years to discover that it had very little to do with my husband at all. When I looked deeper into this, I found that it had much more to do with my past than my present. As a child and as the baby of the family, I often spent time alone. I was left to find my own fun as my siblings went about their lives, leaving me hurt and alone, wondering why no one wanted to play with me.

Eventually, my husband and I started to have conversations about my reactions, not to blame our past or each other—just to seek a better understanding. Labeling or dismissing my reactions as wrong or emotional only made things worse. I could continue to be triggered, and Matt could continue to defend himself and be frustrated. Finally, after many failed attempts, we listened to understand and spoke to be known. Matt heard me and could then see my need. Now when we go out on a Friday night, we both know that this trigger can occur. Just because we have a better understanding, doesn't mean it won't ever happen again.

Matt is now aware that if we get separated, the trigger could happen. Therefore, he is more intentional about making sure we stay together. We can even use humor to acknowledge this, not to belittle or minimize but to help ease the stress that the trigger has caused. Building repeated positive experiences and avoiding the negative builds our intimacy.

Have you been tasked with making a bridge or another structure using only glue and popsicle sticks? In the times that I [Ellen] would do this, the structure would also be weight tested to see if the structure would, in fact, hold up under pressure. The most memorable time I had doing this was when I was a counselor at a camp. One structure was amazingly strong. Each team would submit their project for weight testing. They would add more weights and eventually the structure would fall. For the last structure, even though they added more and more weight, it held up. At last, the youth pastor asked for my team partner to stand on the structure. He was very hesitant to do this but when he got on, there was a brief look of relief as the structure stood. Then there was the look of shock when it fell! Thankfully, it wasn't too high, and no one was hurt in the exercise.

We can look at stress in the same way. Sometimes what seems like the slightest thing can cause the bridge of our emotions to give out in a way that we did not expect. Stress builds up gradually, so much so that we might not even notice it. We are still standing strong on the outside. We can stand on that bridge and it continues to stand strong for a time. Then the term stress fracture comes to mind. We can withstand far more than we could imagine until we encounter a certain situation. Then we find ourselves at the breaking point. We may break in different ways and at different levels of intensity. A breakdown doesn't necessarily mean mental breakdown in a hospital or with a counselor. It may mean a good cry, snapping out at others, or giving someone the silent treatment.

Sharing your challenges with your spouse can lead to less stress. Whether it is a Friday night date at Walmart or a public youth event, we are now able to share our burdens with each other. The benefit of sharing is two-fold. We understand ourselves better so we can receive comfort and healing. We can also better understand the actions and reactions of our spouse. Acknowledging what happens for both parties does not minimize the hurt of either. While they may not be able to solve the situation, understanding can help take the pressure off. Going back to our popsicle structure, the structure was better able to bear the weight by spreading the burden over many parts.

Consider Jesus who was about to face His most difficult challenge and all His friends could do was bicker. Jesus gave us an example of how He responded to them in patience and understanding. It is interesting that Jesus then called out Peter. Peter was someone who often opened his mouth before what he said passed through any type of filter in his brain. Rather than hearing what Jesus said in Luke 22:31-33, he plowed right into a solution in verse 33. Jesus interceded in verse 32 and prayed,

> "Simon, Simon, Satan has asked to sift all of you as wheat. But I have prayed for you, Simon, that your faith may not fail. And when you have turned back, strengthen your brothers." But he replied, "Lord, I am ready to go with you to prison and to death."

Perhaps the greatest example of stress in the Scripture is when Jesus goes to the Garden to pray prior to His crucifixion. The narrative in Matthew 26:36-46 provides some critical information about how we define and the best way to handle stress. We need to acknowledge stress *will* occur, not question whether it will. As the passage indicates, even Jesus had to navigate stress. In verse 26 we see the first action our Lord took was to seek out a time of prayer. What was about to happen later that night was not a surprise to Him, so He needed to prepare. During their previous times together, He had shared with The Twelve what was about to happen. Of course, the disciples did not believe Him. They still assumed that the primary purpose of His mission was political freedom from Rome. Their reactions would have been much different had they really listened to what He was telling them and asked for more understanding. Their expectations were far different from reality.

They were hearing what they wanted to hear which rein-forced their assumptions. Jesus, however, had a perfectly clear pic-ture that led to His stress and what needed to happen. He also took a few men with Him who were part of His inner circle and asked them to pray as well. Then Jesus explained what He was feeling. It should not escape our notice that Jesus did not even invite all 11 who had followed Him just Peter, James, and John. Verse 38 states, "Then He said to them, 'My soul is deeply grieved, to the point of death; remain here and keep watch with Me.'" Stress can be de-fined spiritually as a soul experiencing and processing deep grief and anguish.

The next part of the exchange is interesting. For some reason in the middle of His time of prayer, He reached out to His friends. Of course, they were sleeping and not doing what He needed them to do. He did that not just once, but a second time. The prayerful support and direct fellowship of His closest friends were so import-ant that He sought them out multiple times even though He had a significant direct relationship to the Father. Just as we saw in the Garden between Adam and Eve, an earthly relationship with other people is needed even when direct fellowship with the Father exists. When our spouse is dealing with stress, our first step should be to recognize the signs and listen.

Jesus had a physical reaction to stress which should have been obvious to Jesus's inner circle. The disciples still didn't comprehend it even when Jesus told them He was stressed. He asked for prayer, but they had fallen asleep. This begs the question: Are you listening to your spouse, actively looking for physical evidence and doing what they need rather than what you need? Jesus needed them to pray. Are you recognizing and doing what your spouse needs or are you falling asleep on the job?

Not to give the three a pass, but they had struggles of their own. Their struggles were understandable, but they still failed Jesus in that moment. When was the last time this was true for you, that a person close to you just didn't get it? They didn't see or hear you. When that occurs, it seems to make matters worse because they should know us well enough to know what is going on and then want to help.

In a somewhat surprising move, Jesus asked the Father if He could be excused from going to the cross. He wanted to know if there was any other way around what needed to happen. We should notice that we are in good company when our prayers are not answered in the way we ask or want them to be. The passage did not record an audible "no" from the Father. The Father may not answer us when our stress stays high and something unpleasant is about to happen. Jesus did not get a pass, and neither will we.

The good news is that what Jesus was about to face will not be something we will have to experience. Luke 22:43 reports, "An angel from Heaven appeared to him and strengthened him. And being in anguish, he prayed more earnestly, and his sweat was like drops of blood falling to the ground." The bloody sweat was a physiological indication that the weight Jesus was carrying that night was overwhelming. We might be persecuted and martyred for our faith, but we won't have to take the weight of saving a sinful world on our shoulders. His shoulders are wide and strong and able to handle that significant of a challenge.

Our spouse is our closest friend and the primary partner in our inner circle and support group. The relationship Jesus has with the Church is a picture of the type of relationship a husband and wife share. That is why this passage is instructive and relevant to the topic at hand because Jesus showed us how to properly manage stress. How should we respond when our spouse is the one enduring stress? How should we respond when our spouse is causing stress?

The story is also instructive because Jesus teaches the disciples the best way to respond. However, let's go back to the narrative of The Last Supper first. Jesus has just once again shared with them some news that at the time did not necessarily look or sound positive and the disciples totally miss it. Rather than calling them out or defending His cause, Jesus lovingly shares with them the best way to handle, and how to not handle, a situation when someone is stressed out.

Luke 22:24-27 tells us,

A dispute also arose among them as to which of them was the greatest. Jesus said to them, "The kings of the Gentiles lord it over them; and those who exercise authority over them call themselves Benefactors. But you are not to be like that. Instead, the greatest among you should be like the youngest, and the one who rules like the one who serves. For who is greater, the one who is at the table or the one who serves? Is it not the one who is at the table? But I am among you as one who serves."

There are multiple lessons to be learned from these passages.

1. The first is to acknowledge that there is something going on and the need to pray. This night was not the first night Jesus had talked about what was about to happen.

2. Our assumptions can impact whether we react or respond.

3. Praying for each other when both you and your spouse are stressed will help bring empathy and comfort, although, like in the case of the disciples, it might take some time.

4. Determine that the first and best thing to do is to pray and have someone else praying for you.

5. Don't let blame or shame add to your stress because you ask for God to let you out of your circumstances. It is permissible to ask out. Know that He will give you the strength needed if the answer is no.

6. When you ask for the prayers and physical support of your close friends, it will give you the courage needed to continue in the Lord's will.

7. It is important to persistently communicate what you need with your spouse. Feeling guilty often keeps us from seeking out what we need.

8. After seeking help from our earthly brothers and sisters, it is important that we go back to the Father in prayer.

Our stress and how we handle it are influenced by the expectations we have. When our expectations are met, life is good. When they are not, we can be triggered, and then our relationships become more challenging. Understanding how our expectations are formed helps. Let's discuss this further in the next chapter.

MARRIAGE MATTERS TOOLS FOR CHAPTER 8

The purpose of these exercises is not to add additional stress, even though there is a good chance they will. I [Matt] do have to confess that I remember taking marriage classes that intended to give class time to implement what they were teaching. White knuckles gripping the table did occur, hoping that they would run out of time teaching before giving us time to apply the lesson. A strange reaction, right? I was just going to be talking with my wife. We want you to continue to practice the skills of reflective listening by asking the following questions of each other.

1. Is there a specific situation that is causing stress? Is it keeping you from talking with your spouse?

2. Use the words on the list of emotions to describe how you are feeling about the situation and the stress it is causing.

Now, switch roles as time permits so you both will have an opportunity to be speaker and listener.

EVALUATE YOUR PROGRESS

1. What did you learn about your spouse?

2. What did you learn about your own emotions and perspective

3. Are you motivated to do this again with another topic?

DIGGING DEEPER INTO CHAPTER 8

This chapter's Word search is
stress

Isaiah 41:10

Hebrews 13:5b-6

Deuteronomy 31:6

Psalm 34:4-5

CHAPTER 9

EXPECTATIONS – WHERE DO THEY COME FROM?

*The two greatest challenges in marriage are how we manage stress
and the expectations we have of ourselves and our spouse. The
best way to handle stress and expectations is to understand our
emotions—how and why they operate and what we can expect
when they are healed and under the Lordship of Christ—through
a biblical lens. We engage them to find comfort and healing
through sharing with our spouse.*

How do we define expectations? We have them for ourselves and others. Others have them for us. Our first memories in
life have an impact on our expectations even now later in life.

As a young boy growing up in Pittsburgh, then called the
City of Champions, during the '70s understandably would become

a baseball and football fan. One of that kid's first memories was sitting in his living room watching his favorite team come back from being down three games to one in exciting fashion to win the World Series. His favorite player hit a decisive, long home run late in the game to seal the win. Today, I can see the side arm motion of the pitcher releasing that last pitch. Center fielder Omar Moreno, who regularly made defense look easy, camped under it with ease. After squeezing the ball for the last out in the 1979 season, he and many others jumped as high as they could while screaming for joy at winning baseball's greatest championship.

Earlier that season, my favorite player on the team signed a baseball that I still have to this day: "To Matt, All the Best. Willie Stargell." Their theme that year was "we are family." If you grew up during that time, you likely are hearing that catchy tune in your head right now. Not only was the team a family, but they brought the city and so many of the surrounding communities together. Our family's joy for that time was amazing for that nine-year old lad.

A friend of mine and I [Matt] were at one game late in the 1990 season against the Mets when the Pirates won with a late-game home run. After that hit, we had the desire to scream louder and jump even higher than before. For some reason, my feeble attempts at expressing my elation did not feel adequate. It is then understandable with all the positive experiences that I had in my life regarding the Pirates that I would want the best for them, realizing that the Pirates were my first love.

Then came the fall of 1992 and the Pirates were about to make another World Series appearance. The date was October 14, 1992. It was to be the next greatest event in my lifelong passion as a Pirates' fan. The Pirates were a powerhouse and couldn't lose. They could hit and pitch as well as the best teams. They won 96 games that year and were well on their way to the championship—or were they?

A not-so-fast former Pirates player had something to say about that. As clearly as I am looking at the computer screen upon which I am typing, I can see one of my favorite Pirates chugging around third base and sliding just under the catcher's tag. He won the game for the Atlanta Braves. I could not believe it. I was devastated, and even though the game went late into the evening I called my then fiancé. My expectations of a World Series win and subsequent celebration were dashed (and I'm still recovering more than 30 years later).

Ellen's Expectations

When I [Ellen] was seven, I was living in Cleveland. I had no expectations of any of our teams winning championships, but we nevertheless had expectations, some of which emerged around the holidays. When I was seven years old, my grandmother suggested we go to a place named Kraynaks. It's hard to describe but think of a nursery for plants, add a department store like Target, add on a Hallmark store and a candy store and a train store, and you may be closer to picturing this experience. In short, you can buy just about anything at Kraynaks and certainly we have done a lot of Christmas shopping there over the years.

While this is a treat, and something not to be missed, that is not what is special about Kraynaks. Each year, Kraynaks puts up a Christmas tree display. The display is free, exhibiting 50 to 100 decorated trees, each with its own theme. People line up outside to get into that display. Since the time I was seven, our family has gone every year. When I was a young college student, I took my new boyfriend, now husband of thirty plus years. Since then, we have brought our kids, and they are bringing their girlfriends and friends and now we have our grandchildren going too. This has become a huge family event, one which we plan for and make sure everyone has on the calendar months before to be sure they can come.

When we visit, we follow a certain routine. We drive to Hermitage, PA the same way each time. Before stepping foot into Kraynaks, we go through the Avenue of 144 flags, just next door to Kraynaks. We all tour and try to stick together going through the Christmas tree display, then we go shopping throughout the rest of the store after that. We spend a lot of money in Kraynaks, and while we have lots of Christmas decorations, there always seems to be one more to be found while browsing.

After we spend a couple of hours in Kraynaks, we go to a specific restaurant for dinner named Eat 'n Park. We go to the same restaurant every year with no exceptions. We can't wait for our trip to Kraynaks to come and we are sad when it is over for another year. Sounds idyllic, right? Here's the thing about expectations. Even though Kraynaks is a great place, those very high expectations can cause problems.

There was one year, not too long ago, when we ended up going a second time. Why? As our family grows larger, it is harder to stick together, or to meet up when three different cars are needed. It all felt scattered. Once or twice we tried a different restaurant. Nobody liked the experience, so we went back to our tried-and-true way of doing things. Because I have so many high expectations, even a great trip can leave me feeling a bit disappointed because in some ways it did not meet my ideal and perfect expectations. But when I stop to think about it, an experience should not have to be perfect to meet my expectations. I can have an expectation of having a lovely time with my family and enjoy the day in the moment and in hindsight for what it is, not what I imagine or hope it to be.

Expectations are defined as believing that something is going to or should happen a certain way. They are influenced by our past, our hopes, and our dreams. They can be formulated through what happened positively or negatively in the past. They are influenced according to how we perceive and process what happens to and around us. Some of them are fun, like Matt's desire to see the Pirates win. Many are more serious, like the ones we have about our relationships with others. We have all been disappointed or let down when our expectations are not met.

Have you ever had those you care about most not meet your expectations? If only you would have done this or said that, then you would be "happy." I would imagine everyone has had people in their life who did not perform to our expectations. We are willing to guess that there are more than a few of us who have not met the expectations of those we love as well. Some of our expectations we can verbalize, others we cannot. We may not be aware of the effect our expectations have on us.

That statement may sound a bit judgmental, but there is a reason we may not fully understand. Many of us look back and think our childhood was normal. We assume that others think, respond, and react like we do. That is how we learned, what we experienced. The conflict comes because others have the same perspective on their experience, which feels normal and right to them. This is a concept that will come up several times throughout our journey. We repeat it because it is so important to have a deeper understanding. If you have not dug deeper at this point, know that you are in good company. We had not either. We did not see a need to dig deeper into something that we felt and assumed was normal or common.

Those patterns of thought are most often different from those of others and that leads to conflict or pain.

This is especially true in our primary relationships with a spouse, significant other, parent, or child. Misunderstanding happens when that which feels normal to us gets challenged by another who also feels their polar-opposite perspective is normal. We are all unique individuals, created by God, and we have a lot in common as to how we learn and develop. The more we learn to understand both of those truths, the more intimate our relationships will be.

What to Do?

When we get married, we have a template, a certain set of expectations with which we carry with us. If we have not learned to speak the language of emotions, that experience will be made more difficult as we encounter someone else with a different perspective. This tends to intensify over time as both spouses strive to have their expectations met. Frankly, the only solution will be to stop and learn to think differently, allowing ourselves to see the world through our spouse's eyes. It's easier said than done, but it does work.

When individual expectations and perspectives come into conflict, we must be willing to temporarily put aside ourselves—Jesus called it dying to self. We must be willing to listen and comfort each other, helping our partner carry their cross at that moment. Doing so in no way minimizes our perspective or concerns. We may not even trust at first that our spouse is going to give us a chance to share our perspective. Both the listening and the speaking side of our roles are needed. If your spouse cannot hear you to the point that they will not let you share, that is more of an indication that their pain and hurt go deep. It may indicate that some additional time of them speaking and addressing their expectations is needed.

Don't feel the need to go it alone. A counselor or a trusted friend may be needed. Be careful though, when sharing with a close friend because you are only sharing one side of the situation and your one-sided story may influence their response or advice. Think about the woman who was accused of adultery in John 8. The religious leaders brought her but protected the man she was involved with, which meant his role was not addressed appropriately. We don't want to publicly air our dirty laundry, so to speak, but meeting with someone who is more objective and has less history with both parties in the marriage might bring a much-needed perspective change.

Unmet and misunderstood expectations are responsible for most if not all the conflict we have in our primary relationships. The expectations we bring into a relationship shape how we respond or react. Those that are victims of trauma will experience all this more intensely than others. Those expectations are either met, or they are not. Either way, our expectations are often reinforced in our adult relationships. We will find, however, that the expectations we have because of our childhood cause problems in adult relationships. Continue to read and we will show you some truth that will help to reshape and transform your expectations.

MARRIAGE MATTERS TOOLS FOR CHAPTER 9

We will be using reflective listening in all the remaining tools. Our goal here is to begin to understand the source of the expectations you and your spouse have about one another in your relationship.

1. Take a few minutes to think about some positive stories from your childhood that influence your expectations.

2. Before you begin to share, sit with your spouse in a way that will enable appropriate physical touch that is comfortable for both. Be in a position where you will be able to look into your spouse's eyes and genuinely listen without distractions.

3. Listener: Listen to understand not to judge or persuade.

4. Speaker: Speak to be heard, not to be justified concerning your rightness.

5. Go as long as you want or can. Set a time limit if needed to make sure both of you will have equal opportunity.

The questions are:

1. What are some of your past experiences that contribute to your expectations of today?

2. What activities are relaxing to you?

3. What do you like to do as a hobby today?

EVALUATE YOUR PROGRESS

1. What did you learn about your spouse?

2. What did you learn about your own emotions and perspective

3. Are you motivated to do this again with another topic?

DIGGING DEEPER INTO CHAPTER 9

This chapter's Word search is
blessing

Proverbs 13:12

Isaiah 43:19

Proverbs 19:21

Luke 6:35-36

CHAPTER 10

EXPECTATIONS IN MARRIAGE

*The two greatest challenges in marriage are how we manage stress
and the expectations we have of ourselves and our spouse. The
best way to handle stress and expectations is to understand our
emotions—how and why they operate and what we can expect
when they are healed and under the Lordship of Christ—through
a biblical lens. We engage them to find comfort and healing
through sharing with our spouse.*

We have listed a considerable number of expectations below.
It's not meant to be an exhaustive list but enough to keep us busy
for hours or more like days, weeks, or months. Don't try to tackle
too much at one time. Ellen and I would regularly start our time
together and an hour later would still be discussing the first question
or comment. It also can be valuable to discuss these by what we call

machine gunning the list. Start with the first question and respond with the first 10-15 second answers that come to your mind. Then when you are all done, pick the answer that most surprised you both and dig deeper.

The thought of talking with your spouse for an hour could be an intimidating one or stir some emotions that will be hard to process. Many, Ellen and I included, have been there in our relationship. I am so pleased as a marriage mentor now to say to you that there is hope for you to have better understanding and perspectives. Take things slowly. If one of you can only handle five minutes initially, then that is okay. Do five minutes. If that is too much, don't give up, start with less time. Be patient.

We are going to ask you to push through just a bit after that and add a little more each time as you move forward to grow. If you are comfortable with five minutes today, up it the next time together to 10 and so on. That's the best way to grow and change. Be comfortable, but not completely comfortable. Lines 16 to 20 are left blank so that you can write in relationship-specific questions that will help you understand the expectations you each have in your relationship that are not covered in the first 15.

1. How do we care physically, emotionally, and spiritually for each other?
2. How do we spend our time together?
3. When and how do we spend time apart?
4. Do you believe the other person in the relationship is as invested as you are?
5. Do we understand how and why our spouse reacts or responds to us?
6. Do we understand how and why we react to each other?
7. What are our desires in physical intimacy?
8. When we have a difference of perspective, how do we navigate it?
9. What do mutual understanding and compromise look like?
10. Do we respect our differences?

11. How important is quality time?
12. How important are acts of service?
13. What resources, if any, do we use to build our relationship?
14. Does looking at marriage material help?
15. Does looking at books mean a sign of weakness?

16. _____

17. _____

18. _____

19. _____

20. _____

Many of us looked at these and other topics during premarital counseling. Back then, we found that we were very similar. The results from the personality and compatibility tests we took had our graphs lined up quite nicely, a promising start that provided a sunny outlook on our marriage—all of the graphs, that is, except one. This one thing would be a source of conflict and irritation over the course of our marriage. The busyness of work, managing a home, taking kids to activities including church youth groups, and volunteering in service make revisiting these difficult issues the further along we get into our marriage. We pursued other activities that filled our schedule because we wanted to be involved and engaged in the lives of our kids and community.

We have a check list of priorities written, even if it's a mental list, that we mark off daily, weekly, monthly, and yearly. Where on that list does the priority of our marriage and primary relationships fall? Is it on the "will get to it someday" section of our checklist? Life has a way of messing up our schedules so we feel like we don't have time now. Maybe later? Does later ever come? Then we blink and our kids are driving, going to proms, or looking for colleges or careers, and that person we fell in love with has changed and is completely different. If we are honest with ourselves, we have changed too.

It is far easier to recognize the needed change in others than it is to recognize the need for change in ourselves. Someone said that if we want to understand where our priorities are, we should first look at our checkbook or in our case today, our online bank accounts. That is also true of our calendars. For many of us, carving out the time to read this book or attend a potluck dinner to receive some encouragement or a time of rest is a great challenge.

Have we so focused our priorities on other things so that it is not possible for us to see or feel our own needs? Whenever an opportunity comes up to work on our relationships, are we ready and willing to take it? We can and must break that habit of busyness. The truth is that our busy schedules can be used to deflect some things we need to address. Even cursory glances at the repeated challenges we face with each other can be shoved aside in favor of other things that are in and of themselves important, but do not address our highest priority needs.

We recognize that many of the heated discussions we have with our spouse, parents, kids, or others occur primarily because our expectations are not met or, even worse, not heard or even considered. A reaction or lashing out can seem unreasonable and irrational and perhaps it is. However, the likelihood that it is about the expressed primary topic stated in the intense reaction is not as likely as we might think. Maybe an intense discussion is what is needed. Or maybe if we just told the full truth when we spoke and learned to understand when we listened, we might come to understand why our expectations are important. We have taken the time to understand each other's expectations and the history behind them in our relationship. It does not short circuit every argument, but it does help to lessen the frequency and the duration. It is a lot easier to be supportive when we don't feel attacked or accused.

Why are so many challenges caused when expectations are not met? Is the issue that they were not met or is the primary issue that they were not understood? It can be both. The origin of our stress can be found in our emotions, which we will look at in the next chapter. The next step before that, however, is to look at the Chapter 10 tools.

MARRIAGE MATTERS TOOLS FOR CHAPTER 10

In this next set of tools, our goal is to begin to understand how our emotions and history influence our expectations. This time we want you to start alone with the Lord. Pick one or two of the marriage expectations at the beginning of this chapter for the purpose of discussing them with your spouse. However, let's add another component to this exercise. Use two words from your emotions word list that describe how you are feeling about these expectations. They may be positive or negative. After spending time in prayer, share those two with your spouse after stating the expectation you want to discuss.

Then bookmark this page so you can come back to it at another time and repeat the same process until you have gone through all the expectations listed and any new ones you've found along the way. Once again, use the reflective listening skills you have been practicing in the previous tools.

When it's your time to listen, do so to understand, *not* to judge or persuade. When it's your time to speak, do so to be understood and heard, not to be justified in your rightness. Go as long as you want or set a time limit so both of you will have an equal chance to listen and speak.

EVALUATE YOUR PROGRESS

1. What did you learn about your spouse?

2. What did you learn about your own emotions and perspective?

3. Are you motivated to do this again with another topic?

DIGGING DEEPER INTO CHAPTER 10

This chapter's Word search is
priority

Luke 10:38-42

Galatians 6:9

Deuteronomy 6:5

Psalm 90:12

CHAPTER 11

EMOTIONS MAKE SENSE

The two greatest challenges in marriage are how we manage stress and the expectations we have of ourselves and our spouse. The best way to handle stress and expectations is to understand our emotions—how and why they operate and what we can expect when they are healed and under the Lordship of Christ—through a biblical lens. We engage them to find comfort and healing through sharing with our spouse.

When addressing a difficult subject, we find it beneficial to inhale as deeply as possible and exhale as slowly as possible to help us relax. If the thought of discussing emotions, yours or your spouse's, causes stress, breathe deeply and exhale slowly. Repeat as needed. It will help you to relax and have a better frame of mind.

Emotions are a part of the stress and pressure we experience.

Emotions have a bad reputation in some Christian circles. They are relegated to second-class citizenship status because we often take notice of them primarily when there is an issue or problem. We can feel that strong emotions are a lack of faith or a sign of immaturity. We shouldn't focus too much on them because they are not the primary theological truth of Scripture or part of the gospel message we are commanded to share. Or are they?

There are more than 3,000 words in the English language that describe emotions. Webster defines emotions as

a: a conscious mental reaction (such as anger or fear) subjectively experienced as a strong feeling usually directed toward a specific object and typically accompanied by physiological and behavioral changes in the body;

b: a state of feeling;

c: the affective aspect of consciousness feeling.

The most important thing to remember is that emotions or reactions are not a mini dive into atheism or doubt. Our negative emotions are not an indication that we have lost our faith or are necessarily involved in sin. Jesus himself often took time with His inner circle to help handle His emotions, none of which were sinful. His emotions were never more evident than when He was in the Garden prior to His arrest, as referenced previously.

Scripture and our faith require us to embrace our emotions to help us understand ourselves, others, and the Lord. Look at David in the Psalms. At times, he was a mess emotionally. It is a good thing he was, and also important that he took the time to learn about and understand himself. David's psalms were not just theological, they were emotional full of anger, joy, despair, disappointment, and discouragement. It was David's ability to deal with his emotions that drew him into a deeper relationship with God.

We have roughly 73 Psalms out of the 150 that were penned emanating from David's struggles. David was willing to be called out when he was wrong because he understood his struggle, and he often took it to the Lord. His prayers and concerns were not communicated perfectly. Yet even with all his failures, God still called David "a man after His own heart." We miss an opportunity to understand and let God do His work when we minimize what we feel and/or are unwilling to learn how. We minimize our emotions and then we rationalize why they can't be dealt with.

When I first started this journey, I [Matt]could verbalize three emotions: sad, angry, and, when those two were not in play, a subdued happiness. It was subdued and muted because my shame made happiness short-lived which then made long-term happiness more difficult. The truths needed to address this challenge are in Scripture, but they take a little bit of digging and application to find and then help.

Emotions can be negative or positive. Some of us are more emotional than others. There is no doubt, however, that all of us are emotional beings to various degrees. Some can engage emotions appropriately. Others ignore and deny them out of fear. Others ignore and deny them because they were never taught how to effectively engage and manage them. Some of our fellow brothers and sisters filter their emotions so those emotions are never understood, reach others, and, more importantly, given to the Lord. Imagine that. We resist being fully truthful with the Lord who created us and knows everything about us.

It's interesting that we withdraw even from Him just as Adam and Eve ran and hid from Him in the Garden after the fall. Do we believe He is not big enough to handle them? Do we feel engaging the Lord emotionally would be disrespectful or improper? How many of us pray as if our words will be broadcasted and used live on Sunday morning? My silent prayer time during services looks and sounds a whole lot more like a conversation two people might have at a bar then one might have leading a worship service. It is okay to have that type of brutally honest conversation with the Lord. It is more than okay; it is needed for healing.

In fact, it is far more beneficial than the formal prayer requests where we can "machine gun" before a quick amen. He already knows what we need. Our need to be honest is far more important than our desire to be publicly proper. We are not saying that we have the mouth of a sailor in a weekend worship service. What we are saying is that the best way to heal is to be fully honest and not to hold back with the Lord. The Lord can handle it, but can we handle honesty in ourselves or in others? Or are we too easily offended or protective of our private time? If David, in his time of stress, can ask the Lord to torture and slay his enemies, I think we are okay with a "swear word" or two in our own private prayers. Their use works because they are an honest description about how we feel.

Emotional filters for some are much thicker than for others. Others don't restrain their emotions because they don't know how to express them effectively. There are several places we need to go to understand how we react to people and circumstances, including and especially our personal relationship (or lack thereof) with Jesus Christ.

If I [Matt] am honest, I hang out in mostly Christian circles. A common refrain in those times is that we spend time focusing on the theology of our sin, how fallen we are, and the process of our salvation. We should spend some time there theologically, but there is another side of the coin at which we should look. While thoughts of our sin, depravity, along with God's grace, love, and mercy are true and factual, they don't give us the whole picture.

Before you scream heresy, let's all take another deep breath. Exhale and repeat a few more times. When we feel better, it is easier to be open to what the Lord must show us. How do all those theological truths make us feel? Our hearts are desperately wicked and far from Jesus. Hebrews 4:16 says that we are to approach the throne of Grace with confidence. I am guessing that our first moments in heaven will not be a verbal exam on the theological implications of sin. I see it more about how we will experience the Father running towards the prodigal son when he returns as shown in Luke 15:20-24.

> "So he got up and went to his father. But while he was still a long way off, his father saw him and was filled with compassion for him; he ran to his son, threw his arms around him and kissed him. The son said to him, 'Father, I have sinned against heaven and against you. I am no longer worthy to be called your son. But the father said to his servants, 'Quick! Bring the best robe and put it on him. Put a ring on his finger and sandals on his feet. Bring the fattened calf and kill it. Let's have a feast and celebrate. For this son of mine was dead and is alive again; he was lost and is found.' So they began to celebrate."

God places before us an impossible standard but then expects us to understand and then seek a relationship with Him. First Peter 1:15-16 says we are to be holy as the Lord is holy. I [Matt] struggle to make sense of that in my logical mind. That right there is why it is so important that we engage both our emotions *and* our mind in our relationship with others and the Lord. When we let that balance get out of whack, relationships suffer. Thoughts and truth without emotion leave us with a cold, colorless, and bland existence. Emotions without thought and truth leave us scattered, ungrounded, and susceptible to believe just about anything. Both extremes lead to broken and incomplete relationships with others and the Lord.

So how do we find that balance between our emotions and truth? The first step is to study the Scripture. In that spirit, I took *Strong's Exhaustive Concordance of the Bible* by James Strong and did a word search on emotions. I found around 70 words that described the variety of emotions we often feel. Interestingly, when I divided them up between what I considered positive emotions versus negative, the split was exactly down the middle: 35 positive and 35 negative. I found roughly 11,700 verses on emotions throughout Scripture. Interestingly, there were about 2,200 verses that focused on the negative, leaving roughly 9,500 that described positive emotions or emotional situations.

> *Heavenly Father, I am so thankful that I can cast my burdens at your feet. You will sustain me; you will never permit to be moved away from you. Thank you for your power to sustain my relationship with you. There are no words that can adequately describe how amazing you are. Thank you for seeing me and all my past and remembering it no more. It is my prayer that I will be able to do the same. It is in Jesus's name I pray. Amen.*

Let's consider again the example of King David, identified in the Bible as a man after God's own heart. David did not lead a perfect life. He did not hold back from God when it came to his feelings. Another example is Elijah. When we look at Elijah, he basically said he was exhausted and wanted to die. Did God come at that moment and chastise him? Did God punish Elijah for feeling this way? Perhaps it is time to remember those strong feelings in the context of the stories in which we find them. We need to recognize that God gives us grace with those emotions. Be honest with the Lord and the person He gave you as your life partner. Your spouse is a gift from God. Don't leave that gift unopened and sitting under the tree.

So what does that academic and numeric exercise above mean? The Bible says over 365 times that we should not fear. What does it say about other emotions? We are going to spend most of the rest of this book finding out what the Word does say about emotions and how to effectively deal with them. We want to gently remind you at this point that your purpose is to look at yourself, not at the other person in your significant relationship. That includes your two most important relationships, the first one being Jesus, the second is your spouse.

We mentioned earlier that our purpose is not to look back to blame others or perhaps more importantly ourselves. The truth is that we have assumptions about others, many of which are false. It's interesting that we also have assumptions about ourselves that can be false. Do we have assumptions of the Lord as well? It is often easier to hold on to those false assumptions than it is to go to that person or to the Lord and talk about it. There are a variety of reasons for that.

There are some seemingly random questions that initially come to mind as we delve into this world we call emotions.

1. Are there various types of memories and how do they impact our emotions?

2. What is stopping us from diving in and not only understanding our emotions but experiencing them? Let's call those roadblocks.

3. What are some common expressions of how we attempt to fix them in ourselves and others?

4. What does Scripture say about specific emotions?

5. Is it possible to forgive and forget?

6. Is my relationship with the Lord impacted by how I relate with others?

7. How can we change lifelong patterns of behavior?

8. My spouse isn't interested, so what am I supposed to do?

We will only begin to scratch the surface of the answers to these and other questions you will think of along the way. We pray that the next few sections will give you a reference point, a perspective, and the motivation to seek out the answers. There are many roadblocks that make it more difficult. Being able to acknowledge them makes overcoming through them that much easier.

Some will say that emotions are fickle. At first glance, we agree. They are non-verbal memories of reactions that we have learned in our past. That window of time from our past can range from in the womb to just before we picked up this book. This next tool will help us to begin to understand how our emotions impact us. We can only be successful in using a map if we know our starting point. Unlike our GPS that can automatically find our starting location, we need to put some work in to find the origin of our emotions.

MARRIAGE MATTERS TOOLS FOR CHAPTER 11

Our purpose is to begin to see emotions that feel irrational do make logical sense. We will start this tool by asking you to pick one situation or struggle where your emotions feel irrational or are hard to understand. As an example to get us started, let's consider my [Matt] eating habits. My emotions play all kinds of tricks on my decision-making process concerning what I put in my mouth. I can easily convince myself that food helps me emotionally, even though I know logically that the food I want at that time is not good for me. I will want to eat a sandwich at 2 a.m. even though I know doing so will add weight and make getting back to sleep difficult.

Most of the time when that happens, I am not actually hungry and I do need more sleep to help fight diabetes and be more effective during the day. The result is a disconnect between my emotions and the logic I know to be true. That makes my emotions feel fickle and erratic. The truth though is that the emotions that are driving the eating behavior have a source. Understanding where our emotions come from will not stop them from happening. In short, understanding gives me the armor I need to more effectively address them. Our shame in "allowing" those fickle emotions to have as much of an impact as they do is the start of the healing process.

There are often layers that will take time to navigate. Be patient. The process is as important as the goal of understanding. God can show you when you are willing to learn.

1. Like Matt's eating, pick one subject where your emotions do not feel logical. Pull out your word list of emotions and take a moment and list as many emotions as you can recognize that relate to that specific issue. There is no right or wrong answer. Trust that the Lord will recall what He wants to address.

2. After your time with the Lord, share what you found with your spouse. Speak and listen reflectively and use the emotion words. Take time for your spouse to share what they learned about you. Now that you have a better understanding of the source of the struggle, you are in a better position

to respond rather than react when, not if, those emotions surface. If the issue is a source of conflict with your spouse, understanding will give you both a better perspective to respond rather than react to each other. If you are both triggered over the issue, it is important that you take time to intentionally stay in your roles as listener and speaker. Once finished with the initial conversation, then switch roles as time permits so both have an opportunity to be heard and understood.

EVALUATE YOUR PROGRESS

1. What did you learn about your spouse?

2. What did you learn about your own emotions and perspective?

3. If these emotions have been a source of conflict, have you found that source to be more similar in each other than you originally thought?

4. Are you motivated to do this again with another topic?

DIGGING DEEPER INTO CHAPTER 11

This chapter's Word search is
shame

Romans 10:11

2 Corinthians 4:2

Isaiah 54:4

Hebrews 12:2

SECTION 3

ROADBLOCKS TO BEING KNOWN AND PROVIDING COMFORT

It only took me 30 years plus but I [Matt] finally pursued my dream of having an HO model train set in my home. It had been in or on my bucket list for a long time. I had some good reasons for not pursuing it: no time, no money, no space, no experience or expertise. What if I failed? What if the look of the platform did not match what I had in my head? In truth, they were not legitimate reasons but rather excuses. The biggest obstacle between me and my train dream was fear. I allowed fear to become a significant road-block to achieving a desire I had had for a long time.

We are going to spend the next few chapters looking at road-blocks. There are personal stories mostly of our marriage where we allowed our fear or lack of understanding to get in the way of what we wanted. Getting to where we need to go is not always smooth sailing. We create many, but not all, of our own roadblocks. We erect some for others too. The good news is that God has given us a plan, which at times may seem more like a detour. He has given us a GPS that will not fail. Let's look at some potential roadblocks in the next chapters and how to deal with them. You may be familiar with some and would likely have some that you could add to the list.

CHAPTER 12

REACTING OR RESPONDING?

A few years back when my [Matt's] hair was not so filled with gray and my waist was not so thick, I was interested in watching a new movie that had come out and was then broadcast on the greatest of entertainment vehicles of the early '80s, namely HBO. What an exciting day that was when we finally were able to catch up with friends and have cable in our own home too. The desires of a young teenage boy, however, were not always in line with Scripture. The object of my focus did not have anything to do with appreciating the beauty of God's creation. I wanted to watch a specific R-rated movie.

I won't go into the details as to why I wanted to watch that movie, but let's just say many in my friend group had watched it so I wanted to as well. Seems reasonable, right? At least it was reasonable for me and my teenage brain. I tried to watch, but that attempt was quickly short-circuited by my father. There is much

I don't remember about my childhood. Many will say that I was a level-headed, even-keeled kid. However, I wasn't that night. I remember lying in my bed furious that my father would prevent me from watching such a popular movie.

This was not an, "Okay Dad. I trust you and know that you have my best interests at heart" reaction on my part. This was yelling, crying, and had some irrationally angry moments. Well actually, it was more than a few moments. I will never forget what Dad did in that moment. He came up and sat on the side of my bed and listened. He did not chastise me or make me feel bad for wanting to see a naked girl. He listened and calmly responded to what I thought then was my pain. How could I talk with my friends when they could see these kinds of movies, but I can't?

He listened and assured me that there would be plenty of opportunities in my future to watch movies like this one. He was right about that. If only I had listened to his advice from that night, I would have spared my visual mind having to process lots of what became unwanted images. My point is that my dad listened. He responded, I reacted. If only I had learned from that part of the lesson as well.

We respond when we are intentionally being proactive and self-controlled, our motivation being to understand with the best interests of the other person in mind. Reacting is the exact opposite of that. A reaction seeks to defend and protect the individual who is triggered. It is often a selfish attempt to get what the triggered individual wants. We often feel justified in our reactions because they come from a source within us that has its roots in what and under what circumstances we learned about others. Sometimes we believe we have in some way been wronged by another and that may be true. Our perception is that others have hurt us. I was initially hurt by my father's protection, but he was right. The question that we need to answer is whether we have been wronged or are we leaning back on false assumptions concerning the motives of others?

We can respond or react according to our thought process at the moment. It all depends on how we frame the moment when we have an unpleasant encounter. We can allow those angry thoughts from our partial limited view to come out of our mouths, we can intentionally seek understanding and another possible perspective. The one extreme causes us often to lash out through some kind of inappropriate behavior. The other is measured and carried out with purpose. In both cases, our thinking leads to our actions.

Let's look at Galatians 5:13-17. Verses 13 and 14 are a description of what we do when we respond.

> You, my brothers and sisters, were called to be free. But do not use your freedom to indulge the flesh; rather, serve one another humbly in love. For the entire law is fulfilled in keeping this one command: "Love your neighbor as yourself."

Verses 15 through 17 comprise a great biblical description of what happens when we react.

> If you bite and devour each other, watch out or you will be destroyed by each other. So I say, walk by the Spirit, and you will not gratify the desires of the flesh. For the flesh desires what is contrary to the Spirit, and the Spirit what is contrary to the flesh. They are in conflict with each other, so that you are not able to do whatever you want.

Reacting and responding are often in direct conflict with each other. That means the results we get from reacting will differ greatly for those that we get when we respond. Yet, we still react frequently. You can reduce your tendency to react and improve your ability to respond by exercising self-control. There are a few dozen or more Bible verses about self-control from which to choose. Let's look at a few.

1. *Love requires self-control.* "Rather, he must be hospitable, one who loves what is good, who is self-controlled, upright, holy and disciplined" (Titus 1:8).

2. *Love is intentional.* "So is my word that goes out from my mouth: It will not return to me empty, but will accomplish what I desire and achieve the purpose for which I sent it" (Isaiah 55:11).

3. *Love does not react but rather responds.* "Whatever you have learned or received or heard from me, or seen in me—put it into practice. And the God of peace will be with you" (Philippians 4:9). Learning to change from reacting to responding takes time and

practice—and the will to do so. When you put these things into practice, the God of peace will be with you. Think about the primary relationships in your life. When you put the work in, the Scriptures tell you He will bring you peace.

4. *Love does not react in anger.* "My dear brothers and sisters, take note of this: should be quick to listen, slow to speak and slow to become angry" (James 1:9). This is a verse we will see many times in our study that has a wide variety of applications and challenges for us. There is a reason God created you with two ears and one mouth. This is especially true in marriage and relationships. How many disagreements would you have been spared if you took a breath and decided to listen and not fortify or double down on your own position? Too many to count for me.

5. *Love does not lead to divisiveness.* "Cast all your anxiety on him because he cares for you. Be alert and of a sober mind. Your enemy the devil prowls around like a roaring lion looking for someone to devour" (1 Peter 5:7-8). We give the enemy an opening to divide us when we react instead of respond.

Then there are two other things to do to help control the tendency to react.

1. *Acknowledging or taking note of our tendencies, anticipating them before or while they are happening.* Most of us have times when we get to a point of no return. I am not just talking about when we lose our cool and unleash our pent-up emotions on someone. This also occurs when we let our guard down and say a few unkind or inappropriate things to another person.

   On some levels, especially after you begin to study your emotions, you will be able to recognize that the explosion is about to happen and be able to re-direct it, eventually being able to acknowledge and stop when you are long past having the will or the desire to stop. We can learn about ourselves and how, when, where, and why we react, and then put into practice what the Lord has shown us clearly in Scripture. First Peter 5:6 states, "Humble yourselves, therefore, under God's mighty hand, that he may lift you up in due time."

2. *Talk to the Lord.* This is not Sunday morning worship with lots of "thee's and thou's" while using the name of the Lord every third word. This is you talking with Him as you would talk with any other person. He is even capable of handling some harsh words accompanied by significant anger, frustration, and the many other negative emotions that enter our lives. There have been times when I would not want the prayers of my heart to be used in a Sunday morning service. It's not because I don't want people to know about my struggles, but because the language I use in prayer is not going to be found in a church's liturgy.

First Peter 5:7 teaches us to "Cast all your anxiety on Him because He cares for you." Notice that the reason we cast our anxiety on Him is not because He does not know, but because He cares. Do we give our spouses or significant others that same opportunity? Do we believe they care? It would be a better idea to unleash on the Lord first if needed. He is perfectly able to handle our unfiltered barrage of emotions.

When framed correctly, emotional vomiting all over a spouse can be effective, but we need to be very careful on how we set this up. Emotional vomiting can have a positive physiological impact on our brains and alter future reactions. This is true whether we are the one who needs to vent, or we are the one who needs to sit and listen. The listener needs to be prepared and fully understand that the upchucking is not primarily about them and their perspective, thoughts, or actions.

The need to upchuck can help us feel better just as it does when we have a stomach virus. As with a sour stomach, we want to limit how often this type of engagement with our spouse happens.

Perhaps the listeners in your life have not responded well in the past which is why you don't give them the opportunity to do so now. That is an understandable reaction and often bleeds into our relationship with the Lord. Spending a little time on the topic of effective listening and speaking can help both involved be better prepared when this needs to happen.

First Peter 5:8 states, "Be alert and of sober mind. Your enemy the devil prowls around like a roaring lion looking for someone to devour." There are consistent reactions in patterns that can be recognized in ourselves and others. Take the time to learn what they are. When you are alerted to these in yourself and spouse, you can catch your emotions early enough to acknowledge and care for your emotions, which will often short circuit an eruption.

When you understand your reactions, then you can take time to evaluate them and examine if they are beneficial. If I lash out when I'm hurt because someone else is not meeting my expectations, then will that lashing out resolve my need to be heard and understood or will it make my attempts in the future more challenging? Paul wrote in 1 Corinthians 6:12, "'I have the right to do anything,' you say but not everything is beneficial. 'I have the right to do anything' but I will not be mastered by anything." You have a right, but are you making it more difficult and therefore keeping yourself in the place from which you would like to move on and grow? Second Peter 1:5-9 states,

> For this very reason, make every effort to add to your faith goodness; and to goodness, knowledge; and to knowledge, self-control; and to self-control, perseverance; and to perseverance, godliness; and to godliness, mutual affection; and to mutual affection, love. For if you possess these qualities in increasing measure, they will keep you from being ineffective and unproductive in your knowledge of our Lord Jesus Christ. But whoever does not have them is nearsighted and blind, forgetting that they have been cleansed from their past sins.

Galatians 5:22 then provides us with a picture of someone who is responding in faith to the need for self-control: "But the fruit of the Spirit is love, joy, peace, forbearance, kindness, goodness, faithfulness, gentleness and self-control."

To close this section on self-control, let us leave you with one final thought from Galatians 5:24-26. "Those who belong to Christ Jesus have crucified the flesh with its passions and desires. Since we live by the Spirit, let us keep in step with the Spirit. Let us not become conceited, provoking and envying each other." We can push each other's buttons. Are we treating others unjustly when we react? Yes, we are. We provoke, then defend, and attempt to change the other person rather than ourselves when we react. We can rationalize this because our spouse may not be treating us fairly or justly. We often forget in the moment that they are likely in a similar struggle as we are.

An improved understanding when these triggers occur leads to a change from a negative experience to a positive one. Our memory, whether we can verbalize it or not, plays an important part in whether we react or respond. We'll look at our memory in the next chapter.

MARRIAGE MATTERS TOOLS FOR CHAPTER 12

To understand the source of our emotions, we want to begin to understand how they impact our thoughts and behavior. Will we react or respond? Toward that end, ask yourselves the following question: Have we been conceited, provoking and envying each other?

We develop consistent recognizable patterns of behaviors when we are triggered. Take some time to consider what those triggers and patterns might look like. Then come together with your spouse and discuss what you see in each other. This might cause conflict. That is understandable because these come from deeply rooted issues from our past.

Think about how your behavior changes when you react? What are the behaviors that your spouse displays when they are reacting? Recognizing that these can help us get to a conversation of comfort and healing faster.

This conversation is to promote understanding not to be another opportunity for blame. If you are used to being blamed, this could be a difficult conversation. It is important that both spouses be given the chance to share. The conversation might involve short-term pain. Having short-term pain though can mean that our long-term pain will be reduced or removed altogether.

EVALUATE YOUR PROGRESS

1. What did you learn about your spouse?

2. What did you learn about your own emotions and perspective?

3. Are you motivated to do this again with another topic?

DIGGING DEEPER INTO CHAPTER 12

This chapter's Word search is
console

Colossians 3:12-14

Philippians 2:1-3

Isaiah 40:1

Isaiah 49:13

THE PERSISTENCE OF MEMORY

Memory is a funny thing. Have you ever had it happen that you and your spouse have a shared experience where you both remember it differently? Oftentimes, the more intense the memory, the more varied the recollection.

Matt and I have that different perspective even though we have a common experience of how we met. He will tell a story about how at a dance, the crowds parted, and there I was an angelic vision that rocked him to the core after which he would never be the same. He will also tell you that he had seen me with our mutual friends and therefore asked for an introduction. Whenever this is brought up, I will say that both accounts can't be true. Either it was a blind date, or it was an unexpected meeting. The continuing story of that time we first met until we finally became a couple has similar twists and turns, with similar holes or discrepancies in each story.

We could conclude either that our memories are correct and

the other person's wrong, or that all our memories are flawed. None of us remember anything as it was. The truth of the matter is far more complex and interesting. Our brains are plastic, malleable, and susceptible to outside influence. In addition, our brains are complex, and beyond what we can understand on many levels. Add to this our own personal feelings, emotions, and experiences, and it is no wonder that we all see the world differently. In fact, it's a wonder that we agree on so many of our shared experiences. This is more reason to talk to our spouses, seeking to understand how and why they see things differently than we do.

My [Matt's] first memory was getting a dog around the age of three. The picture I have in my mind is much dimmer than it once was. I still have the feeling of excitement but a blurred picture in my mind's eye of a black and white Shih Tzu puppy. A physical picture of me, hot and sweaty, sharing a popsicle with the dog a year or two later helps me remember the dog but I don't remember that specific event. We had to get rid of the dog a few years later. I remember the parking lot for the give-away and being up late at night alone crying in my bed, missing the dog who was by then frolicking at a farm with other dogs having the time of his life. It's interesting that I don't have any specific memories of playing with him. The next memory I have that I can verbalize is December 31, 1975. We were preparing to celebrate America's 200th birthday the next year, but I was sad that 1975 was ending.

The memories like the ones I describe above are housed in the left side of our brain. Those are memories that we can verbalize and describe at least some of what was occurring around us. There is another type of memory that goes way back, even into the womb, and those are stored in the right side of our brain. They are called our implicit memories. These are memories that were created before we could verbalize what was happening and therefore, we do not remember them because they are not stored in our brains verbally. We can only remember them through the feelings that occurred and were related to them. We then remember them the way we initially experienced them when something occurs to trigger them. Therefore, they are useful in understanding why we respond and react the way we do.

As we begin to realize this need to understand our spouse, we also realize the need to reach out and understand and experience as children. This has led to many discussions and moments of healing, as well as some need for apologies and humility for us with our children for times when we messed up. These memories are important because they served to shape us and them into who we are.

I [Ellen]have a habit of asking my children regularly about their experience, to the point where they probably think I am a broken record. I asked one of our children about their experience because they had been born prematurely. Studies show that these early traumatic experiences affect the brain in significant and important ways. Why would this have been traumatic? Let's examine the facts that we know about the situation.

The doctors and nurses are there to help. While we know this as adults, a newborn has no such perspective. You come out into an unfriendly environment, one where people regularly stick you with needles. You're cold. You're tired. You just want to go to sleep. This does not continue for hours, it continues for days. Those days continue into weeks and then months as you (the newborn) continue to struggle towards health. Who is on your side in this situation? Who is a friend? Who is going to help you?

We were curious to learn what this child's experience was like. We were not certain that they would have any insight because babies can't remember anything, or so we assumed. However, what this child said blew our minds. It was not so much that they had thoughts or feelings about this, but that they could remember. The one detail they gave me about this was so specific, something I had not nor would not have shared with them. I had no choice but to accept it as one hundred percent valid. A few months later, while we were driving, they began to share again, this time without any prompting. We sat and were amazed as we listened. This child was sharing details about their baby shower, not a shower for her unborn baby, but details of the baby shower that was given for me, their mom, in which they were inside me waiting to be born. They described the details of the house and accurately mentioned that we had Buffalo chicken dip at that shower. Again, I could not deny the accuracy of everything she said, and that she was speaking from firsthand experience.

All our memories are an important part of our experience. Most of us cannot put words to what we experienced prior to our ability to process and then describe using words. God has given both types of memories to us with a specific purpose. When we examine some passages of Scripture, we find verses that talk about God remembering. If it is important for God to do, then shouldn't it be important for us? Hebrews 8:10-12 goes into more detail as to why.

> "For this is the covenant that I will make with the house of Israel after those days, says the Lord: I will put My laws in their mind and write them on their hearts; and I will be their God, and they shall be My people. None of them shall teach his neighbor, and none his brother, saying, 'Know the Lord,' for all shall know Me, from the least of them to the greatest of them. For I will be merciful to their unrighteousness, and their sins and their lawless deeds I will remember no more."

Just as the Lord did with Israel, we have made a covenant in marriage with our spouses. This covenant means we will extend mercy, even when we don't feel like it, and sometimes it means we will love when it hurts. Psalm 15:4 talks about someone who "keeps an oath, even when it hurts." That is true when that relationship is with the Father or our earthly spouse and other significant relationships. The call to remember means that we look back into the past.

Hebrews 8:11 clearly states that we look back to know. This is the important part as far as understanding the application this verse has for relationships. Verse 12 says we look back and extend mercy according to the wrongs of our history. "I will remember them no more." How do we get to the point where we remember the wounds and the sins of the past no more? We do so as we walk out our relationship with the Father but also with each other.

Being available and listening to one another's memories has a huge benefit in healing. We were sitting in the bedroom and Ellen brought up an issue that we had been discussing for 25 years. I [Matt] would like to tell you that I regularly responded with mercy and love during these conversations. Truthfully, many times that was not the case. I could be in the room and do the obligatory head nod or give a "mmm-hmm" response. On my not-so-good days, I would think or even say, "Here we go again. Have we not talked about this a hundred times already?" That seems like a logical statement, and it might even be factually true, but it did not make anyone happy. It was rude and dismissive of my wife. Holding on to that "truth" of repeated conversations clouded my ability to listen to understand. The truth was my wife had something that hurt her and after 25 years I still did not get it. Shame on me, right? Well perhaps, but let's look at this from the Hebrews 8 perspective.

Of course, I was not thinking of that passage at the time, but the tools we were learning were all about implementing God's call to show mercy so we will remember the past no more. We should not be surprised but when we walked through this same conversation using God's mercy in a practical way, something amazing happened. Ellen had a painful memory that needed to be shared and heard. To this day, neither of us can remember the subject of the conversation. We can remember a general topic, but the pain discussed in that conversation, the argument that had held us captive for 25 years, has been forgotten, based on one conversation.

God's mercy provided healing to the point that we, as a couple, no longer even remember the original issue. Twenty-five years was addressed in one conversation because of a new perspective of not looking back to blame anyone or even ourselves but to receive the comfort and healing we so desperately needed. This does not happen instantly with every conversation. Sometimes the Lord uses conversations like that to break not just years, but decades of hurtful patterns.

Our memories are persistent because they stick with us. The positive ones are a blessing. The negative ones contribute to our emotional triggers. Our willingness to accept that the vast majority of our emotional triggers are a result of our memories is important. For years, Ellen shared already how we had a different recollection of the details of how we met. When we first started to share our differences, we tried to correct each other and insisted that our versions were accurate. Then something changed. We began to heal and see our story as more complex and layered. Our story is like Bob Ross paintings: lots of many various colors, bringing out the beautiful in the whole.

MARRIAGE MATTERS TOOLS FOR CHAPTER 13

Things are going to get a little more intense with this exercise because most of us don't really want to dig deep to uncover our pain. We may not even see the benefit. However, we all have something we can talk about concerning this if we are willing. If it is too painful right now, then share it with the Lord. His big strong arms are wide open and more than able to handle anything you throw His way. Part of the healing journey, however, includes sharing this wound with another.

A few chapters ago we encouraged you to find a list of feeling words. Get that list as you begin. It is important that you use resources to help in the journey to look back. It won't be as effective if you don't use that tool.

1. Describe the specific memory from your past where you did not feel you received healing or comfort.

2. Use the list of emotion words to determine more carefully how you are feeling. Select two or three words initially. More can be selected as you share to help gain a greater understanding of your feelings as needed.

3. Share with the Lord what those feelings are. Don't hold back. Nothing you share will break His love, acceptance, or compassion for you.

4. Share with your spouse. Your purpose in how you communicate is to be understood, not to blame. Keep the focus on the speaker's pain, not the role of others.

5. Milan and Kay's guide for the listener, located on their www.howwelove.com website, is helpful to walk through questions as to how to understand and lead towards sharing what is needed for comfort and healing. It can be found in the "Free Resources" section on their site.

6. What would healing look like?

7. Are you willing to have God hear you directly or

would you allow Him to work through others He has placed in your life?

EVALUATE YOUR PROGRESS

1. What did you learn about your spouse?

2. What did you learn about your own emotions and perspective?

3. Are you motivated to do this again with another topic?

DIGGING DEEPER INTO CHAPTER 13

This chapter's Word search is
remember

Deuteronomy 32:7

1 Corinthians 11:24

Revelation 3:3

Ecclesiastes 12:1

CHAPTER 14

"I WANT TO BE RIGHT."

Let's go back and look into the Garden of Eden again. Adam and Eve had taken a bite of the forbidden fruit. God, knowing a break has occurred, was proactively seeking to reach out by asking "Where are you?". He did not need to ask for His own sake but for theirs. We find the entire Genesis chapter fascinating in how it relates to relationships. This includes even Satan's exchange to entice Eve and her plea to Adam to take a bite with her. Nothing that was said in those exchanges was factually inaccurate. Each of the statements made was true. Yet what happened led to the greatest cataclysmic event that occurred in human history. Adam, Eve, and Satan all wanted to be "right." We likely would agree that being right did not work out so well. We can allow the "truth" to lead us to the wrong conclusion. The truth led both Adam and Eve to a life of blame, division, hiding, cover, and shame.

We don't expect you as the reader to agree with everything we have written, nor do we want you to do so. Our unique experiences mean that God is working with us differently than He is through yours. We often believe that something God is doing in me should work in others. We have seen, however, how our differences challenge and even distort or limit our thoughts and perspectives. Differences do not automatically mean conflict, hate, or phobia as many in our culture would like us to believe. As you know, I [Matt] am a baseball fan and have virtually no interest in basketball except when I was first dating my wife and needed material to sound knowledgeable in discussions with my future father-in-law. My interest in baseball does not say anything negative about basketball. It is okay that I am not passionate about it like I am about the Pittsburgh Pirates.

Unfortunately, the concept of all or nothing has seeped into the Church and our interactions among believers. Avoiding engagement with others who are different is just as destructive, maybe more so than having an intense disagreement. This is especially true in marriage. Differences do not mean that one perspective is wrong and the other is right. That is often the rub. We want to be right after all, isn't "rightness" the truth? If I am right, then my perspective is true. Or is it?

Multiple perspectives can be true at the same time, even though they are quite divergent. There are times when we do not have all the facts and truth about a given issue. There is a time and a place for clarification of those issues when we need to learn the particulars of a topic. This will be hard for some to accept but having all the truth or facts and sharing them may not be the right thing to do when we are talking about relationships.

What we are talking about here is something much different. We learned that there is a difference between truth and being right. Our perspective or how we perceive what is going on around us is based more on how and what we experience than the actual truth. Most of us have positive motivations for how and why we engage with our spouse and others. We are well meaning. We don't always respond in a way that matches our intention and the actual truth of a situation. We are taught by culture, parents, and even sometimes the Church that messy emotions should be labeled as unbelief, only addressed with a counselor, or dealt with quickly if at all. It breaks our heart when we hear in our classes that brothers and sisters say their previous church experience would have resulted in judgment had they shared their struggles. We label ourselves and others who display emotions as crazy, emotional, or weak. We assign labels because our judgment is the result of a lack of effective understanding.

Our emotions and reactions are not about being right. In fact, one of the best ways to grow is to understand that our emotions are logical. They may not seem logical or rational at first when we or others manifest them. We may believe that ours make sense, but that is because we have processed them a certain way tens to hundreds of thousands of times in our lives. However, even if we don't see them as based in logic or truth, we can come to a place where we accept and understand. That is true for our own emotions and those we see in others.

We need to move from the desire to be right to an understanding of why we and our spouse react the way we do. Our desire or "need" to be right is influenced by our perceptions and our assumptions. Not surprisingly, the Bible has a few things to say about that. The question then is how can we push past our perspectives and assumptions? We are continually amazed at how practical biblical truth answers that question.

We often judge based upon the external, whether that is through physical beauty or the behavior of an individual. First Samuel 16:7 states, "But the Lord said to Samuel, 'Do not look at his appearance or on the height of his stature, because I have rejected him. For the Lord sees not as man sees: man looks on the outward appearance, but the Lord looks on the heart.'" Jesus has an advantage in that He knows our hearts because He is God. The fact that we do not have that same ability does not give us a pass that exempts us from understanding and knowing. In fact, it should motivate us to be more intentional to know our heart along with the heart of our spouse.

Isaiah 42:20 (ESV) says, "He sees many things, but does not observe them; his ears are open, but he does not hear." What are we missing through our perceptions? Our thoughts and assumptions should lead us to question our confidence. Jesus understood this when He perceived the thoughts of some of His followers. He knew that we had questions, so He answered them saying, "Why do you question in your hearts?" We can easily deal with the doubt of what's in our heart first and foremost by remembering that there is no condemnation for those who are in Christ Jesus.

Since Jesus will not condemn us, then neither should we condemn ourselves or others. We will make the same mistake again and again, thinking this time our spouse will hear or understand. This leads to a recurring pattern, or as we call it, the dance that never changes. When in a dance, if you want to change the pattern, you must communicate with your partner and initiate the change yourself. It's true that you can try to change the direction of your partner without notice or by force, but you will end up bumping into one another and stepping on toes. The same is true in marriage.

It is important to remember that our journey is not about blame. Many of us know that when we are being honest with ourselves. However, being honest with ourselves can be just as difficult at times as it is being honest with others. This is true whether we are looking back to childhood or to something more recent. That young child that you were did not have the tools, experience, or mental, physical, and emotional development to process emotions as adults do. It is just as important to forgive and offer comfort to your child-self who is trapped in the past as it is to yourself as an adult.

A desire to be right, whether intentional or not, harms our relationship for several reasons that Scripture highlights. Matthew 7:3 cautions us, "Why do you see the speck that is in your brother's eye, but do not notice the log that is in your own eye?" We will further address the detrimental impact that judging has on our relationships in a later chapter. The short answer to consider here is that judgments of ourselves and others build walls that make pursuing and seeing the truth more difficult.

Proverbs 18:2 says, "Fools find no pleasure in understanding but delight in airing their own opinions." Not surprisingly, we believe our own opinion. We are not fools in this case. We all tend to look at Bible verses like this and not examine them. We gloss over them quickly, thinking they only apply to someone else. It is the partner that is across from you at the dinner table who is the one in need of change. You may know your part but they are the ones who need to change most for you to change as a couple.

We form an opinion that we assume will be helpful to our spouse. Then we are all too willing to share our perspective and try to "fix" our spouse, rather than looking inward. We further assume if our perspective works for us, then it should work for others. Do we really listen or do we jump to conclusions prematurely before understanding completely? If we jump too early, what are the emotions driving that reaction? It is a defense mechanism or deflection. When we do that, we seize control of the conversation, thereby making it easier to avoid what is really going on in us.

On the surface, the Bible using the term *fools* seems a bit harsh. If we take a step back from our own situations where seeing the truth can be more clouded and difficult, what this verse is saying is true. It is foolish to make assumptions that are often wrong and then dig in or double down when the results of those assumptions don't get the change we expect or when they are proved to be erroneous. Only the truth will set us free, not opinions or wishing something to be true. That truth is found in Scripture, but it is also found by going below the surface in relationship with one another.

Paul wrote in Ephesians 4:2-3, "With all lowliness and meekness, with longsuffering, forbearing one another in love; Endeavoring to keep the unity of the Spirit in the bond of peace." Unity and peace are common terms we hear in Christian circles. Do we really know what they mean and how to achieve them? First and maybe most importantly, unity is not sameness or uniformity. That's easy to say, but not so easy to navigate in our personal relationships.

Even when we acknowledge our current and past brokenness, there is a sense that how we react, positively or negatively, feels normal and safe. Research even shows that those who suffer significant trauma sometimes find more comfort in the pain of that trauma than the thought of starting a journey of healing. Yet, if we are more comfortable where we are, how are we to achieve unity and peace? The journey of healing will force us to deal with things that on the surface could lead to division and a lack of peace. It seems almost counterintuitive. The reality is, however, that if we don't step out and engage others, we will never achieve the unity we crave.

Proverbs 18:13 (NLT) states, "Spouting off before listening to the facts is both shameful and foolish." I love this translation because it highlights the folly in speaking and responding when we don't really understand how to listen. "There is not enough Bible" in what others are saying is also a common refrain. At the risk of sounding defensive, although those concerns are understandable, they just aren't true. It is important at this stage to understand that Scripture is our primary source of truth. That does not mean that there are no other sources of material not found in one of the 66 books that are also true and useful. Of course, the material in other sources need to be put through the lens of Scripture before a proper application can be applied. We don't want to be foolish in how we apply it.

The need to be right is problematic for several reasons as we have seen in this chapter. What are you feeling when the desire to be right controls your conversations? We want to be right whether it is with any conflicts with our spouse or our stated theology.

Supplemental truth that is biblically verified adds to our ability to apply truth that is not specific. Let's stop for now and take time to dig deeper into the shame that causes some of the roadblocks to healthy relationships both with each other and with the Lord. One of the results of an over-the-top need to be right are "you" conversations. We will dive more deeply into that in the next chapter. First, resist the temptation to skip the application and examine this chapter's marriage tool.

MARRIAGE MATTERS TOOLS FOR CHAPTER 14

Let's take some time to continue to evaluate your skills as a speaker and a listener.

1. Using the challenge that Proverbs 18:13 presents, think about when you spout off and must share your perspective rather than listening to your spouse. If you and your spouse are regularly interrupting each other, that is an indication that you have a need to be "right." The need to be right can be a big hurdle to navigate.

2. Pull out your list of emotions and pick two. What are you feeling when you react to a situation that begins with you taking over the conversation with another person so you can establish your "rightness"?

3. If you have had training on engaging more difficult emotions with classes like Milan and Kay Yerkovich's "How We Love" Comfort Circle, then pull out those resources and walk through the steps.

4. Ready for the not-so-shameless plug? Reach out to us at marriagehouseministries@gmail.com and we will get you signed up for the next available class to help with your current struggles.

5. Until then, you can use a prop like a box of Kleenex to make sure the one holding the box is not interrupted and the listener is listening without distraction. Having the Kleenex there will also help when the tears come. Don't resist them, for they are a part of the God-ordained healing process.

EVALUATE YOUR PROGRESS

1. What did you learn about your spouse?

2. What did you learn about your own emotions and perspective

3. Are you motivated to do this again with another topic?

DIGGING DEEPER INTO CHAPTER 14

This chapter's Word search is

being defensive

Proverbs 18:13

Proverbs 19:19-20

1 Peter 5:5

James 1:26

Matthew 26:52-54

"YOU" CONVERSATIONS

Let's look at an annoying communication pattern we refer to as a "you conversation." A "you" conversation goes something like this. One spouse begins a conversation by saying, "you" and then proceeds to say something derogatory or critical of their partner. Then the other spouse counters, "well, you," and so it goes. A slightly different pattern starts with "you," which is then countered by the "Here we go again" defense. Trying to be right and force agreement takes so much more time and energy than trying to understand. It took us 25 years to understand how "you conversations led nowhere except to a frustrating, predictable, and ineffective pattern of defensiveness.

Let's look at how we got there and what you can do to improve your conversation. The first "you" conversation started in the Garden. Adam and Eve ate from the tree and God called them out. Of course, since they had been in perfect fellowship with each other

and God, we might think that they would be able to take responsibility and own up to their behavior. That was not the case. Adam
blamed Eve and Eve blamed the serpent. Not much has changed
since then.

The "you" conversation does not work because you are blaming your spouse for your own troubles and inability to handle the
wounds you carry. When you are emotionally triggered, you fall
back into old patterns of blame and defensiveness. If you have the
same repeated arguments with your spouse, do you ever wonder
why your spouse never changes? You may think, "If I say this to
them one more time, then they will finally get it," but they seldom
do.

It is important that you resist this temptation to repeat what
you have said countless times over the years. What you did to others
or what they did to you, no matter how long ago, is still as real to
you and them as when it happened. You conversations indicate that
the struggle with those wounds is current and triggered in your
mind again. Focusing on the facts while ignoring the seemingly
"irrational" feelings around the facts will only add fuel to the fire,
not diminish it.

How do you respond to these conversations? Many mount
a defense. You may attempt to persuade and provide proof of your
perspective's rightness. In your mind, logic provides support for
your assumptions. At this point, one of you is probably emotionally
triggered and thus not likely to effectively deal with facts, especially
when those facts include accusations. The best way to deal with
wounded emotions is to listen without judgment and offer comfort.
Listening without judgment is not giving the speaker a pass. It is
giving them an opportunity to heal and change. Only then will the
wounds have less power.

Healing

We have concluded that our emotions are neither fickle nor
inappropriate. The primary source of those emotional reactions until they are addressed is historic implicit memories. Our reactions
and how we deal with them might seem to be irrational, but uninvited emotions originating from our experiences makes a lot of
sense. Implicit memories are ones that we cannot verbalize yet have
a great influence on us just like those we can verbalize. They are

both stored in the brain, but in different places. We have a responsibility to share and appropriately address both types to help in the healing process. Blaming others is a deflection that will stop us from healing our own wounds.

Healing in the physical body does not begin until the wound itself is addressed. The first part of healing is to "clean up" the wounds by understanding them in ourselves. The second part of healing is to feel heard and understood. We can stay in our "right to be right" or we can lean in and help our spouse by better understanding their reactions. How we do this is important.

We don't invite our negative emotions, but they come anyway. The reason is that they are left unresolved in our brain. Our negative emotions are often learned responses from our past that have gone unchallenged and unresolved. Some of that we remember and can describe. Much of it we cannot, especially when we are triggered and erupt quickly. When we deal with memories we can verbalize, we can use logic and truth. *When we deal with our implicit memories, we need to address our emotions with understanding.*

"You" conversations are never easy and are rarely productive. They can be changed, however, by learning to listen to understand rather than to fix. That is not as easy as just "do it" or "you need to." That is true whether you are the one who is reacting or the recipient of the tirade. They can be made more productive by speaking to be known and not to blame—and listening.

Isaiah 58:9-11 is instructive of how to confront the temptation of the "you." This passage also looks at what happens when we do.

> "Then you will call, and the LORD will answer; you will cry for help, and He will say: Here am I. "If you do away with the yoke of oppression, with the pointing finger and malicious talk, and if you spend yourselves on behalf of the hungry and satisfy the needs of the oppressed, then your light will rise in the darkness, and your night will become like the noonday. The LORD will guide you always; He will satisfy your needs in a sun-scorched land and will strengthen your frame. You will be like a well-watered garden, like a spring whose waters never fail."

Finger pointing and malicious talk is the Biblical definition of a "you conversation. Getting rid of them is easier said than done. If both partners are not willing to participate, then put all the focus of the conversation on yourself. "Honey, Sweetheart, I am beginning to realize that I have not done a good job listening to you. Can we talk about that?" Then be ready not only to be vulnerable, but also to endure a verbal barrage.

Grace enters when you remember that your partner is wounded and hurt just like you are. Give them the grace you want them to give you. Trust that at some point in the future the roles of speaker and listener will be reversed. This new type of communication could be a big ask and a huge sacrifice at this point, but it is worth it. Whether either partner can articulate it at all in their minds or in speech, both have hurts that are still there. You both find that it is easier to lash out and protect yourself. Protecting yourself does seem easier, but there are far harsher long-term consequences. You can be uncomfortable now, or even more so later.

"You" conversations involve lots of assumptions. You probably know what assumptions do to you when you don't recognize them. Let's look at assumptions next and I [Matt] promise not to lead with that three-letter word "you." Well, maybe.

MARRIAGE MATTERS TOOLS FOR CHAPTER 15

It would not be all that unsurprising if you are not fully on board with this perspective change. After hearing this for the first time, we did not believe it either. These tools need to be used with a large helping of grace and mercy. We found that even with knowledge of these new tools, it was easy to revert to old habits and mindsets. When, not if, this happens, remember to show grace.

1. Pick a topic from your recent past that typically ends in a "you" conversation.

2. What you are going to do differently is to be intentional in using your listening skills to understand and your speaking skills to be known. If you don't agree or even understand another's feelings, you can still understand how the stated feelings can make the speaker feel a certain way. When you are the listener, resist the urge to save, fix, or change the speaker.

3. Once completed, switch roles. If there is no time immediately available, respectfully schedule or commit to another time soon.

4. Pray and ask the Lord to search your heart and mind. It won't take long for Him to show you something that needs to be addressed. He does this not in judgment but in love. His goal is healing.

EVALUATE YOUR PROGRESS

1. What did you learn about your spouse?

2. What did you learn about your own emotions and perspective?

3. Are you motivated to do this again with another topic?

DIGGING DEEPER INTO CHAPTER 15

This chapter's Word search is
help

Matthew 7:1-5

John 14:14

Psalm 34:17

1 John 4:18

CHAPTER 16

ASSUMPTIONS MAKE . . .

Proverbs 18:2 states, "A fool takes no pleasure in understanding, but only in expressing his opinion." We often make assumptions about ourselves and others, and they often cause all kinds of havoc in our relationships. The solution is to look at and obey James 1:5: "If any of you lacks wisdom, let him ask God, who gives generously to all without reproach, and it will be given to him." When we ask God and each other for wisdom, we encourage one another and build one another up. The Lord wants us to seek to understand by asking questions and then listening to the answers. When we react, we are not really listening. We are listening with the intent to respond, and when our brain is forming the response, we can easily miss what the other person is saying. We are thus placing our opinion or personal perspective ahead of the needs of our spouse. We may even attempt to encourage one another with good intentions, but like Job's friends, we will come woefully short and look foolish.

For many years, I [Ellen]initiated "you" conversations we discussed in the last chapter. To say I didn't realize I was doing it would be an understatement. I have a lot of emotions, but my issue is that for many years, I was undisciplined. I would spout off about something that was triggering me and, here's the interesting part, I would blame my husband for those feelings. Many times, they had nothing to do with him.

When I did this, Matt's natural defenses would engage. He would say, "No, it's not like that" or would more often say, "Here we go again." As any familiar dance goes, the next steps would be equally predictable. I would repeat myself multiple times, often ending our encounter with angry tears, and one spouse or the other would turn their back to the other in bed or not speak for the rest of the night. But here's something else I would do: I assumed I knew my husband's motives. That is one of my problems, I am an emotional creature. I assumed I knew the emotional subtext in a conversation, both his and mine. My husband has said more than once that I can carry on a conversation by myself, talking and then assuming his response.

How often do we assume the worst in the motives of our spouse or others? When we do so, we waste all kinds of time and emotional energy. We rehearse in our minds a future conversation we are convinced is going to happen and plan our response. We dig in and make sure we have every possible defense ready to utilize. Some of us can create this defense quickly, even as it is happening. Others spend too much time in rehearsals. There is nothing wrong with practicing to organize and understand your thoughts. Doing so can lead to a more effective conversation. What we are talking about here is obsessing by allowing it to take up too much thought time which then leads to stress and distraction. Too much focus can provide a spark when the conversation starts which leads to a word explosion and ineffective communication.

Over the last few years, our family Sunday morning tradition is intentionally eating breakfast together before going to church. After years of getting up early and taking young kids to church, we decided that being able to get up on a Sunday morning and have a leisurely breakfast to allow larger amounts of time to get ready is a good thing. We would like to write that each Sunday morning was a Hallmark moment. Unfortunately, that was the exception not the rule. To say we were the Sunday morning family that had to wear its fake happy face when arriving at church was true. As soon as the tires of the cars rolled over the entrance of the parking garage, the Sunday smiles appeared. In fact, sometimes they did not appear until the car door closed after parking. They stayed in place most weeks until the car wheels ran back over the parking lot exit on the way home.

Most weeks the primary morning meat we enjoy is bacon or sausage. One of our daughters developed a liking for sausage biscuits and gravy. One Sunday morning, we committed to go to the early service. So I [Matt] was not too upset when the dog woke me about 15 minutes before I was scheduled to awaken. After addressing the dog's morning need to go out and come in again quickly, I decided I would get a jump on breakfast. What happened next was both instructive and illustrative. Our dishwasher had broken the night before which I was reminded of by the stack of dishes in the sink. The drainer takes up about a third of the available space we have on our counter.

My [Matt] love language is "acts of service." So getting up before I need to makes sense and is a win. It gives me time to get a head start on what physically needs done. It should be enough to win extra good husband and daddy points in my mind that I am willing to sacrifice much needed sleep to start the day early. The "benefit" of a small house and a kitchen that is in earshot of the master bedroom is that if the person in the kitchen handles the dishes, the chance that the person in the bedroom will hear and wake up is pretty good. That was the case this morning as Ellen woke up and decided to join me in the kitchen.

When I heard her moving around, I rushed to dump the baking mix for the biscuits into the bowl. The reason is because Ellen will often come in and take over my food prep, and I don't like it when she does. Apparently, she thinks I don't have the knowledge or skills to successfully make a delicious breakfast. Not surprisingly, our cooking process differs. I clean as I go; Ellen not so much. So Ellen arrived and I was successfully multi-tasking my way through the kitchen and food prep I wanted. As usually happens, she started asking me questions and making statements about what was happening because she doubted my ability to successfully prepare breakfast. That was my assumption anyway. The result is rarely good when we do that. So what is the other side of the coin, which is Ellen's side of the story?

I [Ellen] woke up to my alarm clock on Sunday morning, which is *not right*. I can't believe I was so short-sighted, I should have remembered that I don't have to get up so early on Sundays. I turned off the alarm and went back to bed. Then I remembered I did have to get up. We set aside Sunday mornings as a special family breakfast time. This is one of the few times during the week when we can get together. We make breakfast each week and this time my daughter had asked for a special breakfast. Plus, I heard plates clanking in my kitchen, hardly conducive to sleep. I got up and came downstairs, mostly not grumpy, but privileged that I would get to make breakfast for my daughter.

I found my husband in the kitchen clanking plates and following a recipe. Naturally, he had looked at this recipe, or some form of it, but I felt that on-the-spot cooking meant for some changes and additions, which I gladly jumped into doing—thus ignoring the recipe. We had a few new things going on and I needed to make sure things were right, which meant ignoring the recipe.

This is a rather predictable routine. I tend to show up in the kitchen, with the purpose of spending time with my husband. After all, what else would have me out of bed so early on a Sunday? As it goes, my husband shortly leaves the kitchen, and I find myself alone making breakfast. I had washed a few dishes along the way (how nice of me), but clearly cleaning dishes was not my priority that morning. Then my husband asked me to do some dishes. I groaned and asked myself, *If he wanted the dishes done, and the breakfast done, why was he asking me to do the dishes from another room? Why was he asking?* It was at that moment that his expectations were not my own. Was it possible that even in the same moment, we were living a different story?

This story brings to light several important consequences of assumptions. We both enjoy and look forward to Sunday morning breakfast. It is a fun, positive experience that we both expect to unfold in a certain way. We both have expectations and motivations for how the preparation will go. The interesting thing is that there is no right or wrong way in either of our approaches. They are informed and reinforced by our past. Our motivations are a clear match. We both want to make the best breakfast possible and spend some good positive time with our family.

The conflict is caused because we both feel that our approaches are the *right* way to get to our shared goal of amazing sausage biscuits and gravy. There is an added consequence that occurs far beyond the kitchen. A stressed and frustrated Mom and Dad are not good ingredients for a stress-free table where once again the cycle of unfulfilled expectations spin further away from what we claim we wanted.

After completing this same cycle once again, we decided to take some time to talk about our expectations. That discussion melted away those assumptions so we could better understand. I [Matt]thought Ellen's actions were proof that she doubted me. She thought my actions meant I did not care to spend time with her. We still are not perfect, but our new understanding has short-circuited what we falsely thought was true. Now the trend is reversed. Rather than having repetitive negative experiences that diminish the blessing of Sunday morning, we are building positive experiences that bring us together more closely as a couple and a family.

It takes time but more trust leads to less assumptions, which leads to less triggers. Even in the heat of the moment, we know the other is speaking out of pain or frustration. We have found listening to our emotions rather than correcting incorrect thinking is much more effective. We know that we are not thinking straight when triggered. When triggered, we don't really care that we are not thinking logically. Spending time to understand rather than correct others motivates us to a more reasonable response. When triggered we don't really care about the other's perspective or what they think we should or need to do. Helping us to distance ourselves from the trigger makes us more receptive to what the other has to say.

The good news is those Hallmark picture cards or movie memories are possible if you invest some effort to understand your partner. Remember to listen so you can understand, not to criticize, respond, or change the other person. Some mornings we do the dishes as we cook, others we do not. Fighting on that hill of which way is "right" is not worth sacrificing the ability to meet our more important expectations for the morning. Remember also to speak to be known not to blame. Often our perspective is one of many options we pursue in accomplishing the stated goal. We make ourselves foolish when our focus is more about proving that our assumptions are correct.

Assumptions are always interesting and sometimes difficult to deal with. We have found that in most cases ours are not accurate, at least not totally. They cause us to replay conversations in our heads when we are speaking for or with the other person, trying to convince them we were right. Prior to our conversation when we came to understand the other's perspective, we would think, *If only the other would change, things would be better.* Let's look at that assumption (there's that word again) in the next chapter.

MARRIAGE MATTERS TOOLS FOR CHAPTER 16

Think about something in your life that resembles our Sunday morning breakfast scenario. Where do your assumptions hinder intimacy in your marriage?

1. Pick one to start and then stay on topic. When this first topic is complete, there will be time and an improved perspective to handle others.

2. What are parts of your past that make up the bulk of those assumptions? Use reflective listening to clarify. You don't have to agree here to be effective. In fact, insisting on being right will make things harder.

3. Do you now have a better understanding even if you still don't agree?

EVALUATE YOUR PROGRESS

1. What did you learn about your spouse?

2. What did you learn about your own emotions and perspective?

3. Are you motivated to do this again with another topic?

DIGGING DEEPER INTO CHAPTER 16

This chapter's Word search is
testing

1 John 4:1

James 1:2-3

Job 23:10

Zechariah 13:9

TIME TO CHANGE YOUR SPOUSE

At the beginning of the book, we said that we had great news for those who wanted to change their spouse. Well, the time for that great news is here. Be honest. How many jumped here first after reading the chapter title in the Table of Contents, just like we jump to the sex chapter in other marriage books? We are seeing a stadium full of spouses cheering deliriously as if the Pirates, after decades of futility, have finally won the World Series! As cool as that would be for our spouse to change while we remain the same, the path we have for you may not be what you were hoping for.

The strangest thing happens when we apply the truth outlined in this book: Your spouse will change. First Corinthians 7:14 in the *Berean Study Bible* says, "For the unbelieving husband is sanctified because of his wife and the unbelieving wife is sanctified because of her husband." Biblically speaking, the key to changing your spouse is to change yourself. One of the most powerful changes in perspective for me [Matt] happened when I was once again frustrated because I believed Ellen was helicopter parenting one of our kids. I wondered how many times we were going to bail them out? We had taken many homework assignments, forgotten lunches, or band instruments to school so the kids would not have to experience the pain or the consequences of having forgotten those things. How many last-minute, late-night runs to the store were we going to make (or worse yet when an NFL game was on television)?

In truth, my frustration was more about not being a family effective enough to handle these things in an orderly or timely fashion. A noble desire to be sure, right? As the leader of the home, part of my role is to mentor and lead us to effective time management, skills we need as adults which we should be modeling for each other. Of course, when I am the one who needs bailed out, the primary focus is on how it is okay because I don't need bailed out nearly as often as others. Well, the Lord had a way of changing that false narrative.

We were headed towards our normal dance of Ellen asking, then insisting, and me complaining, then resisting. We have danced many times to the sound of the helicopter parenting song. The dance typically ends in stepped-on toes and a frustrated partner. That most frequent ending to the song was one that neither of us really wanted but we never really worked to change our dance routine. After all, each one of us is right in our perspectives and that is what matters. If I dare step out of my pattern of accepting that my assumptions are correct, then I would be making the wrong move, therefore hurting my spouse. (Not true, but a false assumption.)

Jesus is the best dance instructor and His next move for me in this story was different. That move was far less painful and took a lot less time. I asked Ellen what was going on emotionally behind her desire to save the kids so often. Her few-sentence answer completely changed my perspective. The understanding that I had gained opened my eyes to see and it happened in an instant. Part of that new vision meant that we each saw the other's point of view more clearly. It is not about being right or wrong but about understanding. Now, I am quickly reminded of her feelings. I see her and the pain that influences her reaction, and I can respond in grace and mercy rather than frustration when I tell her how we should be parenting our kids.

The same is true for her. She sees my motive behind my misguided criticism. We now can more effectively navigate through that conversation, the result being we were both instrumental in helping our spouse change. Our previous approach led to resistance and no change. Our new approach focused on understanding and led to mutually accomplishing our stated goal. Feeling like your spouse believes you are wrong builds resistance and slows down the journey to reach our goal. Now, we often bail each other out. We help one another sacrificially and direct the time we spent arguing to more positive pursuits. Keep in mind, the communication patterns that needed to be changed were developed in the past and reinforced throughout our lives, causing them to be embedded in our personalities. This is what makes them so difficult to change. Any change will take time because we need to reverse years of learned behavior. That's not easy, but it's worth the effort.

I [Matt] was talking with Ellen one time, commenting how I had regularly been frustrated with her over some issue. The great news is that after several years of positively reinforcing communication and understanding, I could not remember the specifics of what caused the conflict. We had had so many positive interactions that they mostly replaced the past negative arguments, so much so that we did not even need to think about our new process or intentionally use our new perspective. We had both learned so well over time that our new approach had been ingrained as our new dance step. From my perspective, my spouse had changed. The practical application of this, however, is that after understanding the emotions underneath that drove my reaction, I was able to better respond. That resulted in both of us being less defensive and reinforces our conclusion that a pattern of positive interactions positively reinforced our relationship and provided actual emotional healing and support.

Managing time and priorities can be a challenge for any couple. We can be so focused on ministry to others that we neglect the most important relationship the Lord gave us apart from the one with Him. There is a time for everything, including preparation and recovery from our busy schedules. Our own time challenge is threefold. The first is a commitment to taking the time to learn something new. The second is to keep the information uppermost in our minds so we can practice our marriage skills until they become second nature. The third is to continue to learn new principles and strategies so we can build on what we have learned previously.

Ellen and I have been Christians for more than 30 years. We attend church regularly, have served in various ministries, and personally read the Scriptures and pray. We did and still do have the occasional "intense fellowship" as our former pastor called it. Yet with all that church experience, why were we still having trouble in our marriage? We seemed to have the same issues repeatedly with no change happening. Was it frustrating? Absolutely. It was a bit embarrassing too.

We would often guess or plow forward in one-sided communication because we had no idea what our spouse needed. We often were unable to communicate what they or we needed. If we don't understand what we are feeling, we won't understand what we need. If we don't understand what we need, we won't be able to communicate it effectively in a way that will help our partner provide the necessary comfort. Before we go back into that endless cycle, there is now hope.

We have learned to take the time to explore what we need. While this can be scary at first, we trust our spouse will be there for us. Add to that, practice, practice, practice. The benefits of being honest with our spouse far outweigh any temporary discomfort that we may experience. As one of us said, "That was not as bad as I thought it would be." We need to encourage a safe environment of sharing. How we listen and how we speak are critical to understanding and growth.

We have learned in our marriage and from other personal relationships to let go of the need to be right and quote facts from one perspective. Listen to understand. Speak to be known. Neither minimizes truth in any way. In fact, doing so opens us up to getting to the core of our conflict for resolution, comfort, and forgiveness. Our relationship has never been better. We have had amazing discussions with our kids. We are all now much more transparent and the conflict between us has reduced dramatically.

It would be nice if the conversations we have with our spouses were able to be done fairly, meaning that we speak and listen to each other properly and effectively. As we have said, if something is true then it should be beneficial when we share it with others—if it is motivated by love and grace. Telling the truth is not using the

Scriptures as a justification or a club. When you get stuck in conversation, it feels cool to try and prove your case. Doing so, though, doesn't produce the kind of fruit that leads to a healthy, growing relationship. You should listen to understand, not to criticize or to change. Speak to be known not to blame.

When we are not honest with each other or when we don't feel like others are listening, we tend to repeat ourselves to be heard. This is otherwise known as nagging. Let's jump there to talk about that in the next chapter. Check out the Chapter 17 tools first.

MARRIAGE MATTERS TOOLS FOR CHAPTER 17

Chapter 17 tools involve a process of having a series of honest conversations. Name one thing that you would like to see changed in your spouse's life.

1. This is a challenge to look at together. Have your spouse tell you what they need.
2. Decide what you can do to change you, not your spouse. Be patient. Listen. Explore to understand. Be intentional about non-sexual touch as your spouse permits.
3. Pray for wisdom and perseverance and watch how the Lord works.

No matter how long it takes, it is worth the effort. The more the positive changes can be seen, the more motivated both will be to continue the journey.

Here are some suggestions to help the conversation.

1. What emotions does that one potential change that is needed to support your spouse invoke in you?
2. Invest time and have patience while dealing with sensitive issues. Remember, you will be tempted to defend or talk your spouse out of how they are feeling.
3. Sincerely apologize for any past hurts you may have caused.
4. Speak honestly and openly about how you feel. Are you willing to make that change even if that change is also a trigger for you?

EVALUATE YOUR PROGRESS

1. What did you learn about your spouse?
2. What did you learn about your own emotions and perspective?
3. Are you motivated to do this again with another topic?

DIGGING DEEPER INTO CHAPTER 17

This chapter's Word search is
blaming others

Romans 2:1

Genesis 3:12-13

Jeremiah 17:9-10

Proverbs 16:25

CHAPTER 18

GITTY-UP!
IS YOUR SPOUSE A NAG?

Nagging. This is something that I [Ellen] do not do. I wish that this chapter, like so many others, would be for other people. But alas, it is mine to write because it's been my challenge during our marriage. At some point, I heard someone say that as a wife, I should present my need to my husband once and then let it go. If I must bring it up again because he hasn't responded, surely that would not be considered nagging, right? Naturally, our husbands would respond immediately and appropriately, Not so fast.

We are all flawed and selfish human beings who often want our own way. This can easily express itself in our closest relationships when our guard is down. Our different thinking and perspectives fuel our need to be right and heard. It is possible that I [Ellen] do

145

nag and that my husband does not always respond positively to what was asked of him.

One more thing about nagging. We often don't even realize we are doing it because our perspective is understandably impacted and influenced by our unmet need. Want a sure-fire way to put distance between you and your spouse? Be a nag and don't respond when you are the one being nagged. To get right to the point, we all nag when we feel like we are not being heard.

In Luke 18:1-7, we read about someone who was a nag.

> "In a certain town there was a judge who neither feared God nor cared what people thought. And there was a widow in that town who kept coming to him with the plea, 'Grant me justice against my adversary.' "For some time he refused. But finally he said to himself, 'Even though I don't fear God or care what people think, yet because this widow keeps bothering me, I will see that she gets justice, so that she won't eventually come and attack me! And the Lord said, 'Listen to what the unjust judge says. And will not God bring about justice for his chosen ones, who cry out to him day and night? Will he keep putting them off?'"

The reason we tend to nag or push for a more positive reaction is that we, or our spouse, need something. The person with whom we are engaging is ignoring our request and that leads to frustration for both parties. What was the judge's reason for refusing? The Scripture does not say. The good news though is that in the present, we can explore those reasons with our spouse. But how we explore is important. What happens when we feel the need to nag? Do we ignore, dismiss, or tell our spouse with a pointed index finger that they are wrong?

The interesting thing is that we often wave that finger literally or figuratively with the best of intentions. My spouse is reacting or verbally saying that I don't care about them. How many times have we been on the receiving end or what we consider to be false accusations from our spouse? All we need to do is to correct their false assumptions and their thinking by telling them the factual truth. After all, the truth is the truth so they should believe it just as I do.

How is that approach working for you? Long term, it never worked for us, or for the many if not all the couples we coach.

Notice that because the judge did not address her concerns by exploring her claims, neither of them got what they wanted and were frustrated. Nothing changed for the better, and perhaps it changed for the worse. Look again at verse eight: "I tell you, he will see that they get justice, and quickly. However, when the Son of Man comes, will he find faith on the earth?" Ignoring the issue does not result in anything positive in the long run. In fact, Jesus' words to conclude the parable were pointed and at first glance not very nice or loving. We can save ourselves a lot of grief by addressing the nagging when it occurs.

So how do we avoid being nagged? At this point it is easy to think that it is the other person who has the bigger problem. That may be true, but the Lord wants to directly deal with our own responsibility. The positive aspect of this is that nagging is rooted in persistence. There are some good things that the Bible says about persistence. There are some good application points for our marriages.

1. God keeps us from temptation (Revelation 3:10).

2. Gives us strength (Philippians 4:13).

3. Gives us hope (Romans 5:4).

4. Gives us an opportunity to practice patience (Hebrews 12:1).

5. "Rejoicing in hope; patient in tribulation; continuing in prayer" (Romans 12:12).

6. Our example will inspire others (1 Timothy 6:12).

7. Helps us to find the truth (Revelation 2:2).

8. The Lord directs your hearts into the love of God, and into the patient waiting for Christ (2 Thessalonians 3:5).

Those eight principles when applied by both the person doing nagging and the one receiving it will help bring them closer, rather than divide as even the most well intended nagging will do. Instead of using the gift of persistence negatively, we turn it into a positive by pursuing our spouse to understand where they are coming from.

Let's apply those eight principles into our marriage relationship. A godly application of persistence keeps us from temptation. When we are in conversations, we can be tempted to go down multiple paths that do not lead to change or resolution. Often we spend hours on a topic and the only thing that happens is we table it intentionally or until the issue triggers one of the partners again. That's frustrating and confusing for both spouses. We are tempted to nag to fix our spouse, to persuade them that their perspective is not the truth, or that the nagger is more right than the listener.

When we practice godly communication techniques, we build strength and momentum in our relationship. When we revert to old patterns, our relationship is weakened. That weakness contributes to future failures even more than the previous ones. The positive momentum gives us hope that our relationship will improve. When our hope grows, we will have more motivation and opportunity to practice patience. Once we see the changes, we will be able to rejoice in that hope continuing in prayer. We will also inspire each other and those closest to us. Their response will encourage us through their words and their change in behavior. Most importantly, the result will be that we find truth which directs your hearts into the love of God, and a better walk with the Lord.

We can be positively persistent. When we are negatively persistent, we become judgmental and rude. If only my spouse would see it my way, things would be better, or so we think. Let's make things better by looking at the impact of judging in our next chapter.

MARRIAGE MATTERS TOOLS FOR CHAPTER 18

This tool is meant to have you spend some time considering where you are in relation to nagging.

1. Are you nagging your spouse? Are you being nagged?

2. Spend some time in prayer. Below may help if you are struggling with what to say to the Lord.

   Lord Jesus, at times I feel unheard, triggered, and emotionally challenged. Search my mind and heart and show me where I need emotional healing and comfort. Lord, I may not feel it right now, but I am so blessed that I have access to a community of people who desire to hear my heart, to understand my pain, and want to help bring me comfort. Lord, ultimately I want the primary person for that to be my spouse. Right now, things aren't going too well, and we are nagging each other and not understanding one another. Lord Jesus, Your love, grace, mercy, and compassion are awesome. I trust You to provide those for us. I also trust that You will use me to help provide that for others. I pray this all in the name of Jesus. Amen.

3. Share with your spouse what you have learned about yourself when you nag by listening and speaking reflectively.

4. Listen to what your spouse has to say about what they found out about themselves.

5. What do you both need to make a change that will help address nagging in your relationship?

EVALUATE YOUR PROGRESS

1. What did you learn about your spouse?

2. What did you learn about your own emotions and perspective?

3. Are you motivated to do this again with another topic?

DIGGING DEEPER INTO CHAPTER 18

This chapter's Word search is
prompt

Ephesians 5:15-16

1 Corinthians 14:40

Philippians 4:9

Psalm 144:4

CHAPTER 19

JUDGE NOT –
OR SHOULD WE?

Remember, most of us believe that how we respond or react to situations is normal and correct. In Matthew 5-7, Jesus delivered what is possibly the most impactful sermon of all time, the oft-quoted Sermon on Mount. This sermon contains one of the most misunderstood passages in all of Scripture. Let's go old school and look at it in the King James Version: "Judge not, lest yea be judged" (Matthew 7:1). How many times have we heard that verse in our lives? Perhaps it was spoken as a warning to you, or perhaps you were the one doing the warning. As someone who has done both, I [Matt] know this verse is often used when someone doesn't want their actions and words questioned so they in essence say, "Don't judge me." They are using this verse as a shield to cover all sorts of behavior, attitudes, and sin.

A quick look at the context of this verse tells us that this application is not accurate. In the Sermon on the Mount, Jesus repeatedly said, "You have heard it said . . . but I tell you." Jesus was exhorting His listeners to look beyond the surface of a matter so they could judge with discernment. It seems that Jesus was talking about not judging matters of the heart, for no one knows the heart but God. In John 7:24, however, He said, "Stop judging by mere appearances, but instead judge correctly" (NIV).

So when and how should you judge, particularly in marriage? *Judging can hurt your relationship when you allow judgments to turn into assumptions.* To address judging, *you need to look deeper* at the felt emotions that are causing the words and actions you are tempted to judge. This presents a challenge since we are not mind readers. We can't accurately do this even if we have been with our spouse for many years and "know" them well enough to complete their sentences for them.

Even when the circumstances or the topics are the same on the outside, what is driving them may be different on the inside. *Having honest conversation helps to avoid the pitfall of an inappropriate judgment and jumping to conclusions.* We are not simply judging by what we see or hear but are working to get to the heart of another person. And when we "judge" that what has happened in the past is happening again now, we have jumped to a conclusion based on an assumption because we made a judgment or assessment of our spouse's behavior without trying to understand their heart.

So what is judgment and what are we doing when we practice it? In our marriages, most of the time we don't evaluate our spouse's word or behaviors because we want to win an argument or help them find a solution to what they are saying or feeling so we can move on. We want for them what we consider to be accurate from our perspective. If we are "judging" them, it is because they have exhibited some kind of stress or emotion which leads to behavior or inappropriate words they expressed. We are judging them because they are not doing something "right."(Basically different from how I see it should be).

Wanting what is best for our spouse is quite a different motive then wanting to win an argument or debate. However, making decisions about and implementing an approach that is based upon the desire for what is best often does not result in what we initially are hoping for. We develop repeated patterns of interaction that don't address the real issue. The reason for that is our "judgment" of external behavior, words, or internal thoughts does not address the real reasons the behavior occurs.

In the last few years as Matt and I have worked at having more honest conversations. I have often found that I need to first question my own reactions and attitudes. Philippians 4:8 applies here once again: "Finally, brothers and sisters, whatever is true, whatever is noble, whatever is right, whatever is pure, whatever is lovely, whatever is admirable—if anything is excellent or praiseworthy—think about such things." This verse invites us to question our own thoughts and reactions and yes, even our judgments. This is another application of Jesus's exhortation to take the log out of our own eye before we judge our spouses. I have found that self-evaluation goes deeper than surface matters.

I [Matt] tend to judge Ellen when she is being overly emotional. I [Ellen] tend to judge Matt when he is being too logical. Being logical and emotional are not necessarily a bad thing. They can be a blessing into our relationship. We both tend to respond to one another out of our own perspective and life history. An appropriate response depends on the needs of our spouse and not our own needs. If our response is to defend our position or correct our partner, then it is better not to respond in that manner. We should respect the boundary they have established. The reality is that we often judge the actions of our spouse and instead of freeing them from their anger or pain, it tends to prolong it along with the disagreement we are having.

When we have taken off our judge's robes, have we accomplished what we set out to do? Most of the time, we will not have resolved the issue when we judge inappropriately but only served to postpone a resolution into the future. We then must circle back and have the same discussion again. The next time it happens and we repeat the same reaction, we will only make matters worse. If we are not moving forward and improving our relationship, we are making it more complicated and problematic.

So let's look at that verse and its context again:

"Do not judge, or you too will be judged. For in the same way you judge others, you will be judged, and with the measure you use, it will be measured to you. Why do you look at the speck of sawdust in your brother's eye and pay no attention to the plank in your own eye? How can you say to your brother, 'Let me take the speck out of your eye, when all the time there is a plank in your own eye? You hypocrite, first take the plank out of your own eye, and then you will see clearly to remove the speck from your brother's eye" (Matthew 7:1-5).

For years my wife and I had the same reactions to each other at the end of each workday. Even though we enjoy working at our jobs, I [Matt] would still come home at the end of the day exhausted, not so much physically but emotionally. Ellen would say that I spent everything I had at work and I had nothing left for her. She was partially correct, but I felt she did not fully understand my perspective. In a sense, we had judged each other when in fact we both had an incomplete understanding of one another's perspective and needs. *We heard what we wanted to hear rather than what the other person was saying.* I had to work hard so I could provide for my family and have the resources to do the things Ellen claimed were important to her. So, after eating dinner (and most often not saying thank you), I retreated to the couch or my room. I was tired so I deserved that time to rest before the next child responsibility or other housework that needed to be completed. My perspective on this issue was a judgment. I placed on her a standard that I was not willing to follow myself. That made me a hypocrite.

Now let's look at it from her perspective. Any mother knows that while parenthood is a blessing, it is not easy. Comedian Phyllis Diller once said that cleaning the house while you have children at home is like shoveling while it is still snowing. At the end of her day, my wife was looking for relief. Her work in our home was just as stressful as mine outside of it. Her work did not end with the same tangible reward such as a paycheck and adult social interaction like mine. Meeting the expectations of children was tough and much more relentless than those in the workforce at a "real" job.

We had both decided before we were married that one of us would stay home so the kids had a parent each day. We were living what we started out to do. Why then were we finding it so frustrating? Every night was the same struggle. At the end of a busy day, we were both tired, stressed, and in need of some comfort to refill our emotional tanks. Add to that our ability and motivation to respond in a fatigued, stressed state was more challenging than when we were well rested and had clear minds and calm emotions.

James 4:11-12 says,

Brothers and sisters, do not slander one another. Anyone who speaks against a brother or sister or judges them speaks against the law and judges it. When you judge the law, you are not keeping it, but sitting in judgment on it. There is only one Lawgiver and Judge, the one who can save and destroy. But you—who are you to judge your neighbor?

The neighbor in this passage is another believer, not someone who lives in a house next door or down the street. However, when you think of it, our closest neighbor is our spouse. We are disobeying Scripture when we judge our spouse without having all the information and we can only get that information through open, honest, and uninterrupted dialogue. How do we address this issue of judging biblically?

1. Acknowledge and start to recognize when you are judging your spouse.

2. Listen rather than defend your position. That's not easy to do when tensions are high.

3. Look inwardly toward your own behavior. Take out the log in your eye before going after the splinter in the others. What is your motivation for judging?

4. Ask questions to find out more. There is a good chance that you are not the primary cause of the behavior you are judging. False assumptions in a relationship are the gas that fuels many relationship fires.

5. Study what Scripture has to say to better understand judgment and when you are engaging in it.

6. Pray that the Lord would give you His perspective of your spouse rather than relying on your own assumption and judgment.

In our ministry, we often hear accusations from one spouse against the other to the effect that they don't care, or they don't love properly. Rather than trying to minimize those feelings of your spouse, embrace them. Ignoring or rationalizing them won't make them go away or lead to healing. It is not about who is right or wrong. Those emotions are present because of something out of the past. Our current emotions come from a variety of sources including interactions with others, neglect, past abuse and sins of our partner. It is important to remember that although our wounds are in the past, we are experiencing them in the present.

Remember that the goal is having positive emotional experiences that build your relationship. After working through the tool, check out the digging deeper section. The verses listed there highlight the consequences of criticizing your spouse because of an inaccurate and unbiblical judgment.

So what are some of the possible judgments that are in play in your marriage and how would Jesus handle them? If we are to be like Jesus, then we should model our response after His. Are you sitting in judgment of your spouse? In the next section, we will start that journey back from the division of judgement to the love, grace and mercy that result from honest conversation.

MARRIAGE MATTERS TOOLS FOR CHAPTER 19

Here are some possible topics to discuss where judgments have turned into assumptions.

1. How important is living out our faith daily?
2. How do we budget and spend our time and resources?
3. What are our expectations for physical and emotional intimacy?
4. Does one of us want sex more than the other?
5. How do we each define social time?
6. How do each of us "recharge" our batteries when we are tired?
7. Staycation versus vacation?
8. Mountains, parks in the woods, or a beachfront house for the week?
9. List as many topics as you both want to discuss that are specific to your relationship.

It is one thing to discuss and understand differences. It is another to not be judgmental when our expectations are being challenged. Here are some tips to help guide your discussion.

1. List the expectation. Speaker: One aspect of the topic only.
2. Reflectively listen and repeat back what you believe you have heard to confirm understanding.
3. Listener: Accept any criticism of your understanding and be willing to change. You are not the primary expert on your spouse's perspective. Remember, the goal is to have a clear and accurate perspective of your spouse, not necessarily to reach agreement.
4. Talk about the feelings that are fueling the conflict over your expectations. It is important for the speaker to share their perspective, not dive into judging and "you" conversations. This is not as easy as it

sounds, especially at the beginning. For those who need help defining how they feel, an emotions word list will help the exchange be more effective and lead to a better resolution.

5. Does the speaker need an answer, a solution, or to be heard? Listener: Ask, don't assume.

6. Listener: Let the speaker share what they need to feel the conversation was beneficial.

7. Come to an agreement on something concrete and tangible. "Spending less money" or "spending more time" is too general. "Don't eat out for a month" or "Tuesday night is a 'no kids date night'" are more tangible and easier to track and accomplish.

EVALUATE YOUR PROGRESS

1. What did you learn about your spouse?

2. What did you learn about your own emotions and perspective?

3. Are you motivated to do this again with another topic?

DIGGING DEEPER INTO CHAPTER 19

This chapter's Word search is

acceptance

Romans 14:1

1 Peter 3:9-10

Romans 15:5-6

1 Peter 3:8

SECTION
4

THE ROAD TO
INTIMACY AND PEACE

Facts don't care about our feelings. However, our feelings shine a light on the facts and help us to better interpret and apply them in our lives. That is true in our secular work, but it is also true in our walk with the Lord and others. Jesus felt emotions intensely, yet He did not sin. He was angry enough to flip tables, sad enough to cry in public, and frustrated enough to swear at others and openly chastise those closest to Him. He was anxious enough to sweat blood.

In each case, those emotions influenced a behavior or action in Jesus, but the action did not lead to sin. We would do well to remember that when uninvited, intense emotions invade our minds and hearts in ourselves or those of our spouse. Rather than react and make things worse, we can, as Jesus, respond in obedience.

I [Ellen] often repeated things because I did not feel that I had been heard the previous time. But the flip side of that is also true. My venting would lead to emotional rants. I would often say things that I should not have said at a volume that was not necessary.

Sharing emotional needs can lead to difficult conversations. They should not be used to harm others in the process of sharing.

Sometimes it feels safer to stay in our pain than it does to step into the process of healing.

We need to confront the roadblocks in our lives. We can acknowledge that some are external, but some are internal and of our own making. Our patterns of reaction can fortify the wall that has been erected. We hope to turn that around and have our understanding of biblically based attachment remove our roadblocks brick by brick.

God gave us human relationships even when we had direct fellowship with Him before mankind sinned. God is all-sufficient to save but there was a reason man being alone in a perfect garden was not good. There is no question that we should rely on our relationship with Jesus. But He also made us to have fellowship with each other. He uses people to provide comfort, relationship, and resolution just as He uses them to share the message of the Gospel: "Finally, all of you, be like-minded, be sympathetic, love one another, be compassionate and humble" (1 Peter 3:8) and "Be kind and compassionate to one another, forgiving each other, just as in Christ God forgave you" (Ephesians 4:32).

God uses this process to improve our limited understanding and to accelerate our sanctification. This is how we change and grow. We have had this conversation with others on many occasions. Someone may say that we simply need to get back to applying Scripture, which is partially true. If this is a "just do it" prescription for pain, how long will that last? Is there really a heart change in that or are we carrying out our religious obligation? I wonder if I have been missing the heart of the Gospel because I am too focused on the work side of it. Those works are important, but they are external. They should be a reflection and a response to God's work in my inner being and not a reaction.

Am I looking to fill a space that only God's relationship with me can fill? I have found that fixing it or having faith that it will go away does not lead to real growth. Paul said I do what I don't want and don't do what I want in Romans 7 and 8. We can find truth in math, science, and other areas of our physical and emotional world. That does not make the application of that truth to be "Jesus and" whatever else we learn. The lens of Scripture enables us to apply truth and be confident that what we are doing is from the Lord. The Bible is all true, but not all truth is in the Bible.

How often do we respond to Scripture as a "to do" list? When we do, we are missing an opportunity to grow more fully in our walk with Jesus. Let's look next at how this applies to marriage.

CHAPTER 20

THE EYES OF JESUS

One night I [Matt] was struggling in prayer. In truth, I am not sure one could consider it prayer. A "whine and cheese" engagement without the cheese would be a more accurate description. I did eventually get to the prayer part and asked God to show me through Jesus' eyes a person who had hurt me. Be careful what you pray for and be ready for the answer. There have only been a few times in my life when I felt His actual presence in a room with me during prayer at this level of intensity. It felt like what is described by Moses when the Lord hid him and permitted a quick view of His back. I will remember that exchange for the rest of my life.

Perhaps you and your spouse are struggling. The most effective perspective change I have had in relation to my marriage is to see my spouse through the eyes of Jesus. I would hope that others would show me that same kind of grace and mercy. Seeing one another as the Father sees us will help us extend greater compassion, love, and understanding to others when they are triggered.

Scripture gives us an outline of how we can make this change proactively. Seeing and responding to triggers in ourselves and our spouse helps us to minimize their intensity. When we do this regularly, we can minimize the intensity for ourselves. When we see them in each other, we can proactively respond rather than react defensively or attempt to talk the other out of what they are feeling. Here are some verses that can help us proactively respond to our loved one.

1. Psalm 34:15 states, "The eyes of the Lord are toward the righteous and his ears toward their cry." Be intentional and seek out what our spouse has to say including their emotions.

2. 2 Peter 3:9 states, "The Lord is not slow in keeping his promise, as some understand slowness. Instead he is patient with you, not wanting anyone to perish, but everyone to come to repentance." Focus on our spouse, then be patient and ready to engage when your spouse is ready. You should desire that your spouse receives comfort and healing first and foremost. You need to be on the lookout for opportunities to help. It is important that you don't push too much or nag. Doing so will not result in the end results we desire.

3. Jeremiah 5:21 reads like this: "Hear this, O foolish and senseless people, who have eyes, but see not, who have ears, but hear not." Take the time to understand and listen. Being foolish and senseless will not help us accomplish what we desire in our relationship with our spouse. We are foolish when we don't heed the next verse.

4. 1 Corinthians 4:5 says, "Therefore judge nothing before the appointed time; wait until the Lord comes. He will bring to light what is hidden in darkness and will expose the motives of the heart. At that time each will receive their praise from God." Seeing your spouse through His eyes will reduce or

prayerfully eliminate the desire to judge. We have seen previously how damaging judging our spouse can be.

5. Paul wrote in Ephesians 4:3 (ESV), "With all humility and gentleness, with patience, bearing with one another in love, eager to maintain the unity of the Spirit in the bond of peace." Your new perspective will bring you peace and give us the patience you need to more effectively minister to your spouse. Your gentle spirit will encourage your spouse to be honest and to feel safe when they share. When your spouse can share and not be judged, increased unity in your relationship will be the result.

The following verses are some of what the Bible says about how the Lord sees us. We addressed this in an earlier chapter but it's good to keep this in mind.

- "For he chose us in him before the creation of the world to be holy and blameless in his sight" (Ephesians 1:4).

- "I have been crucified with Christ. It is no longer I who live, but Christ who lives in me. And the life I now live in the flesh I live by faith in the Son of God, who loved me and gave himself for me" (Galatians 2:20).

The statement that says, "I was getting married, I blinked, and now I am in my mid-50's" is accurate. When I [Matt] was younger, I thought I understood those with more life experience when they said that time goes quickly. I did not comprehend how quickly. I regularly had an "I'll get to it tomorrow, next week, at the end of the school year" mindset.

That mentality, for both of us, led to not much change in our marriage or our relationship with the Lord. Passively going through the motions rather than proactively impacting our marriage and our relationship with the Lord had become issues. How many of us can go to church, hear a fantastic sermon to which we "Amen" all the way through and then 15 minutes after the service have no idea what it was about? This was not about being older and forgetting, because this happened when our hair and faces were still young.

This happens because we take our spouses and even our relation-ship with the Lord for granted. The first eight verses of Ecclesiastes 12 help shed some light on how to and why we should confront this passivity but let's just look at the first verse: "Remember your Creator in the days of your youth, before the days of trouble come and the years approach when you will say, 'I find no pleasure in them.'"

I [Matt] looked up the original language for the word *pleasure* in this passage. The first definition listed in Google was, "Pleasure; hence (abstractly) desire; concretely, a valuable thing; hence (by ex-tension) a matter (as something in mind)." This verse calls us to look back at our youth and remember God and the trouble we had in the past before we no longer find value in either of them. If we find no value, then we will not look back and miss the value of how our past experiences impact us today.

Proactively and intentionally remembering your past is an important component to healing. Perhaps you don't currently have many memories of your past. The Lord will bring those back as you take this journey. It breaks our hearts when we see couples walk away and refuse to engage in this process. The reasons vary but the bottom line is that they are missing an opportunity to have the Lord do sanctifying work in their lives.

Let's continue reading through verse 5 of Ecclesiastes 12:

Before the sun and the light and the moon and the stars grow dark, and the clouds return after the rain; when the keepers of the house tremble, and the strong men stoop, when the grinders cease because they are few, and those looking through the windows grow dim; when the doors to the street are closed and the sound of grinding fades; when people rise up at the sound of birds, but all their songs grow faint; when people are afraid of heights and of dangers in the streets; when the almond tree blossoms and the grasshopper drags itself along and desire no longer is stirred. Then people go to their eternal home and mourn-ers go about the streets.

There are two things that jump out from that passage. The first is the urgency for the need to remember quickly. The second is the reason we don't. Storms will come and the light we had in our relationship will grow dimmer with time. We are both struck by how all-encompassing the fear in the story has become. Even the smallest parts of our lives become a drag to the point nothing stirs us. That paints a bleak picture. Those of us who have made that trip know how accurate that picture will be when we let our fear take over. I almost get a "life is hard and then we die" vibe from this verse. There is good news though if we go back to verse one and remember for then we can bring healing when we do. The birds can and will sing loudly again. This would be a good time to pray:

> *Lord Jesus, I'm often afraid. I often wait too long. I blinked in my youth and now I am approaching my mid-'50s. I wasted a lot of time because I was not willing. Show me today where I need to look back. Give me a sense of urgency so that my walk with You isn't rendered meaningless.*

We need to have a new vision of our spouse because we have lost sight of what we saw when we first met early on in our dating life. Our love-colored glasses affected how we saw our future spouse and gave us exhilarating feelings of love and romance. Our new eyes can help us retrieve and revive those feelings we had back then that we have not experienced for a while. We will explore that phenomenon in the next chapter.

MARRIAGE MATTERS TOOLS FOR CHAPTER 20

In our marriage over the years, we tried to improve and make changes but the changes never stuck for very long. We went right back to our old ways of relating. This next tool will address having a sense of urgency about improving your relationship. The questions to discuss from this chapter's theme are:

1. Are you happy with the level of growth you and your spouse are currently experiencing?

2. What is holding you back from having a sense of urgency?

3. What can each of you specifically do to improve the relationship?

4. On a scale of 1 to 10, rate your ability to listen to your spouse since starting this book.

5. On a scale of 1 to 10, what rating would your spouse give you?

6. Keeping the focus on you and not pointing the finger of blame at your spouse, how does that make you feel?

7. Are you tired of your primary motive in your discussions being the need to be right?

8. What is your spouse's number one need right now?

9. What is your spouse's primary love language?

10. Examining yourself honestly and transparently, what are the primary roadblocks for resisting changes that need to be made?

Ask the Lord to show you your spouse through His eyes.

EVALUATE YOUR PROGRESS

1. What did you learn about your spouse?

2. What did you learn about your own emotions and perspective?

3. Are you motivated to do this exercise again with another topic?

DIGGING DEEPER INTO CHAPTER 20

This chapter's Word search is
loved

Proverbs 18:22

Romans 12:9

1 Peter 4:8

John 13:34

CHAPTER 21

BRING BACK
THAT LOVIN' FEELING

When we get married, we often have a fairytale image of that gorgeous girl or hunky guy but those that have been married for a while know the image fades quickly. A Righteous Brother's song comes to mind that describes the situation:. "You've lost that lovin' feeling." Those of us who have attended any type of marriage conference or listened to a sermon or teaching about marriage will have heard that love and marriage are much more about choice than positive feelings toward your spouse. There is a lot of truth to that.

Just because the original feelings are lost does not mean that you should never invite them back. We often ask couples, "What initially was most attractive to you about your spouse?" Some men say, "She is hot!" (Guys, if you ever need to answer this question, make sure you use the language she *is* hot, not she *was* hot.) "She was interested in me. He was so caring. He had dreamy eyes. He was passionate." Couples are often hesitant to share about their spouse's physical beauty, which certainly played a part in their attraction. The assumption is that those kinds of answers are considered shallow or even not Christian. However, there are no right or wrong answers to that question. It is purely a subjective response.

When we look back at that time and the feelings those reasons bring to our mind, what happened to us physically? Did you get butterflies? Are you even briefly tempted to daydream of those early days? We can remember on some level what those exciting moments were like. Flash forward years later in your marriage relationship and you obviously know that doing the dishes, taking kids to activities, paying bills, and cleaning the house don't arouse those fun physical, emotional, and spiritual sparks that you once experienced. For some, those sparks are out, and the sparkler may have been soaking in cold water for far too long. That is understandable given all the pressures and responsibilities of marriage and parenting life. Like the song says, we've lost that loving feeling

You can, however, capture and cultivate those initial giddy, exciting feelings about your spouse. You are simply out of practice. "Wow, Matt, that just sounds so romantic. But if I love my spouse, won't those sparks come naturally?" No, they won't. In fact, you need to be intentional and talk with your spouse about them. You should not apologize for that. Let me share an example as Ellen and I had an opportunity to go to a wedding of a young couple we had the privilege of mentoring.

It had been years since Ellen and I had slow danced together. In fact, neither of us could remember when it last happened. Of course, if this event was a rom-com, then everyone else in the room would disappear and we would be the only couple in the room. Well, that did happen for a moment or two. Then we, or I should say I, reverted to cranky-old-man mode when the song ended and I and my aging back walked off the dance floor, assuming my wife who knew I did not fast dance would follow. She was still in the moment though and stayed on the dance floor starting to jam to the beat of the next song. She turned around expecting her man to be there, but I had left her alone. Not many good husband points earned for sure.

There are several lessons to learn from that experience. The most important one is to put yourself in situations where you can remove the barriers in your busy mind and allow those memories of young love to return. Not only are they possible, they are also necessary. When you practice that by creating more opportunities for that to occur, those feelings will linger longer and come back more quickly and do so at unexpected times. I learned my lesson and although I did not do much dancing, I did not leave my beautiful bride alone on the dance floor the next time.

Exodus 20:8 says, "Remember the Sabbath day by keeping it holy." We are commanded to remember regularly and to act accordingly. Regularly, in the case of our relationship with the Lord, is going to church one day a week. We may regularly go to church for a week but how much time do we spend with Him outside of church? If you only give the Lord an hour a week, He won't be a priority and you won't grow. The same is true in your marriage.

Repeating experiences like dancing together builds a positive history upon which your bodies and minds will be able to better respond. There is a certain amount of truth that our minds physiologically need different and sometimes increased stimulus to create the same dopamine rush that contributes to those feelings occurring. Our bodies have the ability; they just have not done it in a while or frequently enough. Be intentional often enough and the spontaneous will begin to happen at surprising times.

After spending some time thinking about and feeling the feelings that I had for my wife when we first started dating, they came back as strong and as fresh as they were when we were first dating. It was an amazing experience. I could feel the stress leaving my body. I felt ten years younger. If only the gray hair on my head miraculously disappeared as well as the excess padding around my waist. I have not felt that good since our 25-year anniversary trip when we got away for a few days and were able to relax. It took time for the stress to melt. If we let it melt more frequently, the ice that builds up will disappear faster.

I would not be telling the truth if I claimed that giddy, stomach-churning, excited emotions stayed with me at that same intensity level. They did not. What it did, however, was change my perspective when I came down from that dopamine high. The rush of feeling had gone, but the sense of peace and joy remained. Understanding and capturing those positive emotions help us deal with our circumstances and the reactions of our significant other more effectively. Make the good emotions last longer and bring comfort not self-judgment to the not-so-good ones.

One of the challenges to recapturing those feelings is that we often wear masks that block others from seeing the truth. They are also a great way to hide what is going on inside. Let's look at the masks we wear in the next chapter.

MARRIAGE MATTERS TOOLS FOR CHAPTER 21

Pull out your list of emotion words to look at the positive emotions we desire in your relationship.

1. Describe how you felt when you were first dating. How did that impact you physically? Take time to focus on the positive emotions that occurred.

2. What were some of the activities that you once enjoyed that you don't do now?

3. Did you respond differently in the past than you do now? What are those differences?

4. When was the last time you had that giddy, new relationship feeling with your spouse?

5. What can I do over the next month to give those feelings a time to return?

EVALUATE YOUR PROGRESS

1. What did you learn about your spouse?

2. What did you learn about your own emotions and perspective?

3. Are you motivated to do this exercise again with another topic?

DIGGING DEEPER INTO CHAPTER 21

This chapter's Word search is
passion

Song of Solomon 1:1-4

Song of Solomon 1:9-10

CHAPTER 22

TAKING OFF YOUR MASK

The two greatest challenges in marriage are how you manage stress and the expectations you have of yourself and your spouse. The best way to handle stress and expectations is to understand your emotions—how and why they operate and what you can expect when they are healed and under the Lordship of Christ— through a biblical lens. You engage them to find comfort and healing through sharing with your spouse.

We have looked extensively at the negative aspects of emotions, stress, and expectations. We also looked at how they practically impact your relationship. There is a positive side to all this as well. Understanding both the negative and positive sides of your stress, expectations, and emotions will bring healing and unity in relationships.

None of this is a quick fix. What these principles do, however, is lay a foundation or perspective as well as provide tools to help navigate your emotions and interactions with others when, not if, challenges occur. Those who don't engage their emotions out of fear of the negative or an inability to do so miss the positive aspects of emotions. Your emotions, like the rest of your created being, reflect God's image so you are blessed by taking this road of discovery to understand them. Part of that process is that you will need to remove or change something.

I [Matt] have spent countless hours watching movies. Many are the sappy love stories in which the underdog guy gets the girl. One of my favorite endings to an action-packed superhero movie was *Spiderman 2* starring Tobey McGuire and Kiersten Dunst. Spidey was fighting Doc Ock so long in the final battle scene that he had forgotten Mary Jane was still close by. Peter took his mask off to persuade Dr. Octavius to do the right thing. After that happened, Peter looked back to a stunned MJ in revealing that the Spiderman she loved was Peter. Her look of relief and amazement was emotionally satisfying. It's interesting that there are some relevant applications for marriage to consider from this scene.

Spiderman wears a mask with MJ because he falsely believes that not being completely honest with the woman he loves will somehow protect her from danger. Our masks hide our true selves. Sometimes we wear them to protect someone else. In the comic book series, MJ and Peter eventually get married. Removing the mask helped Peter accomplish what he wanted but failed to do with it on. Wearing a mask may seem like the right call but the mask contributes to the problem. Masks do have their place but not in primary relationships. You need to acknowledge where and when masks are effective and appropriate. When you hide to protect yourself or others, you not only avoid the bad, but you also miss the good.

We are about to get real and dive into a very personal part of my [Matt's] life and thought process that even today plays a part in maintaining my comfort as I seek to understand and fulfill my own emotional needs. Many of the tears I have shed while writing are because I am understanding through exploring emotions that I do have value and specific purpose in God's eyes. Understanding this leads to my willingness to change and allows me to ask God's help in those areas.

The perception of yourself has a powerful impact on whether

you react or respond. I thought while I was younger and in school that a girlfriend or relationship would validate my worth. I was the nice quiet kid who typically had one or two guy friends. My best friend growing up was a few years older, so we did not hang out in school. I thought if someone was willing to see me as boyfriend material then perhaps I would have value.

The truth is that I have value apart from any relationship. The fact that I hid my emotions meant that I was unable to see that. In many ways, engaging my emotions was like a snowball rolling down a steep hill, growing bigger and more unmanageable as it went. Ultimately, the light of truth and its warmth and beauty melted that snowball and stopped its descent. The mask I was hiding behind was gone. That is such a better place to be personally in my walk with the Lord. Things also are much better with my wife. The best way to remove your mask is through honest conversation. The truth does set you free. We will look at honesty next.

MARRIAGE MATTERS TOOLS FOR CHAPTER 22

Let's get started applying what we have discussed.

1. How has this journey through negative and positive emotions affected you?

2. What are the masks that you need to remove to see clearly?

3. What is hindering you from intentionally looking at your emotions? What can you do to address those roadblocks?

EVALUATE YOUR PROGRESS

1. What did you learn about your spouse?

2. What did you learn about your own emotions and perspective?

3. Are you motivated to do this again with another topic?

DIGGING DEEPER INTO CHAPTER 22

This chapter's Word search is
mask

2 Corinthians 3:18

Genesis 38:15

2 Corinthians 4:2

Job 24:15

CHAPTER 23

HONESTY

As Christians, most of us strive to meet the standards of the Commandments. When I went to confirm that "thou shall not bear false witness" was in fact the eighth commandment, the initial list for a search on the Ten Commandments stopped at seven, which did not include bearing false witness or the warnings against covetousness. Perhaps it's a coincidence, but our culture struggles with truth as well as desiring to have what others have materially and sexually. That cultural struggle with honesty has crept into our personal relationships because we don't necessarily have a clear or complete definition of honesty and how to apply it to our daily lives. That lack of understanding about honesty erects significant roadblocks to integrity and ethical growth.

Let's start this chapter with a personal story before exploring what the Scriptures say about honesty and how we can remove those roadblocks that a lack of honesty creates. As Christians, we are to be factually accurate in our engagements with others. We have different levels of relationships, which range from those we don't know who "friend" or "follow" us on social media to our closest two relationships, our spouse and the Lord. It is not necessary to share the full picture with everyone except the Lord. However, sharing in full with your spouse will help with your emotional and spiritual health. Sharing fully with your spouse is part of being honest and can expedite your sanctification.

For almost 30 years, I [Matt] struggled with a particular past sin. Although the Lord and my spouse knew the details of what happened, only the Lord knew how those past sins impacted me in the present. The interesting part is that I had not struggled with this specific sin for 30 years, but the effects of it were still weighing me down. A point that I did not really understand myself. Until I had an honest conversation with the Lord and then my spouse, nothing changed.

I shared with her the guilt I felt because I finally understood its impact. Since sharing it in full with my spouse, it has not been a struggle to the point of not even once experiencing the guilt that it had occurred. I used to believe that only God could forgive and forget. I am learning that honest conversation can result in comfort not just with God but with those closest to us. It leads me to believe that the comfort we receive in heaven will be so complete and comprehensive that we will remember our lives on earth but not experience the sin and pain we endured while here.

A Billy Joel song comes to mind. The name of the song is "Honesty." When you come right down to it, honesty requires talking about yourself. You don't know what is going on in another person's mind or heart, so you can't really be honest about them. As God is the author of truth, you must look to Him to show you the truth about yourself. You will see that the Scripture teaches this kind of honesty is an important part of your faith.

However, being factually accurate is only part of being honest. The heart-breaking words of the song state honesty is such a lonely word because it is hardly ever heard. Honesty is what we need most from our spouse. It was not until I was fully honest with my wife that the roadblocks of my past sin went away. This even after worshiping regularly in church, reading my Bible, praying, and serving in various ministries for decades.

Are we lying to ourselves and others when we don't engage our emotions fully? Yes. Let's look and see what the Scriptures say. Mathew 26:36-38 tell us,

> Then Jesus went with them to the olive grove called Gethsemane, and he said, "Sit here while I go over there to pray." He took Peter and Zebedee's two sons, James and John, and he became anguished and distressed. He told them, "My soul is crushed with grief to the point of death. Stay here and keep watch with me."

Jesus was not married but He did have an inner circle of three with whom He shared His deepest, most intense moments. Jesus knew the outcome of that week. Even what He shared with the disciples at the first communion table was not fully what He was feeling. The application lesson here is that we need to be fully open, but not with everyone. Not being fully honest with your spouse will cause conflict as Proverbs 6:19 states. "A false witness who pours out lies and a person who stirs up conflict in the community." Your lack of full honesty causes the conflict you have in your marriage.

Part of Jesus' preparation for the Cross was the time in the Garden. Scripture says that His disciples had not forsaken Jesus until He was on the Cross. Jesus, who had a perfect and intimate relationship with the Father, still needed a place to share honestly and fully. Seeing that full honesty was important for the disciples' preparation for their journey. They, of course, failed and first fell asleep in the Garden and then scattered later that night. Scripture only records Peter verbally denying Him in fear, but they all essentially rejected and denied Him when they ran, one so scared that he did not stop even after his clothes fell off. They had seen many miracles, including raising Lazarus, yet they still scattered. Ultimately all but one died as martyrs. A big transformation occurred after that night. They remembered what Jesus taught and modeled throughout that ordeal, and it completely changed their lives. Jesus can do the same in you through an open, honest, and intimate relationship with your spouse.

James 1:26 states, "Those who consider themselves religious and yet do not keep a tight rein on their tongues deceive themselves, and their religion is worthless." Full honesty is not regurgitating every thought and feeling that comes to mind. When you do that, you may feel temporarily better but you make everyone else feel worse. James said it well. When we don't rein in our tongue, it leads to deception and aggravation on the part of others.

Luke 6:31 says we should do to others what we would want to have them do to us. Second Corinthians 8:21 says, "For we are taking pains to do what is right, not only in the eyes of the Lord but also in the eyes of man" and James 3:17 adds "But the wisdom that comes from heaven is first of all pure; then peace-loving, considerate, submissive, full of mercy and good fruit, impartial and sincere." What those verses are saying is that being fully honest is not a pass to use your honestly to bash others.

The specific instruction about sharing fully continues in Proverbs 11:3: "The integrity of the upright guides them, but the unfaithful are destroyed by their duplicity." Duplicity is the result of selective sharing, and it results in destruction. Second Peter 3:10-12 says,

> For whoever would love life and see good days must keep their tongue from evil and their lips from deceitful speech. They must turn from evil and do good; they must seek peace and pursue it. For the eyes of the Lord are on the righteous and his ears are attentive to their prayer, but the face of the Lord is against those who do evil.

Full honesty requires attention and a desire to seek and pursue it just as the Lord does when you are in prayer.

Philippians 4:8-9 is a familiar passage. This passage is an excellent definition of honesty:

> Finally, brothers and sisters, whatever is true, whatever is noble, whatever is right, whatever is pure, whatever is lovely, whatever is admirable—if anything is excellent or praiseworthy—think about such things. Whatever you have learned or received or heard from me, or seen in me—put it into practice. And the God of peace will be with you.

After reading these verses, you don't see the words describing this procedure as easy, neat, or proper. Think about the interactions King David had with God in the Psalms. Many of them are not prayers and interactions we would likely repeat at church on Sundays, yet David was a man after God's own heart. David asks the Lord on several occasions in prayer to send his enemies to destruction.

We see in ourselves and the many others we engage in ministry that taking time to understand the background of our differences with the truth is far more effective than "just do it" or whatever other approach we can come up with. Not sharing the truth of the ensuing behavior seems like it's an easier way, but embracing the differences between us can facilitate the healing and the understanding we claim we want to see in ourselves or others. It is counter- intuitive in a way but it works.

Let's end on a positive note. Proverbs 24:26 says, "An honest answer is like a kiss on the lips." The wisdom writer gets a big thumbs up from us on that one. A topic for another time, but physical intimacy will improve when we are willing to be honest and effectively communicate and receive our spouse's emotions. As we come down the home stretch in the book, let's start to put all the pieces together and look at how to achieve and enjoy effective comfort and joy in our marriage relationship.

MARRIAGE MATTERS TOOLS FOR CHAPTER 23

Speak to be known not to blame. Listen to understand not to change or criticize. Don't use questions as a weapon.

Ask yourself the following:

1. Is there a sin that is hindering my intimacy with my spouse? Take time praying to the Lord. Have an honest conversation with your spouse, not to blame or accuse, but to understand the sin's impact on the relationship.

2. What comfort do you need to receive to help in healing this wound?

EVALUATE YOUR PROGRESS

1. What did you learn about your spouse?

2. What did you learn about your own emotions and perspective?

3. Are you motivated to do this again with another topic?

DIGGING DEEPER INTO CHAPTER 23

This chapter's Word search is

honesty

2 Corinthians 8:21

Psalm 139:1-6

Colossians 3:9

James 1:26

CHAPTER 24

EFFECTIVE UNDERSTANDING AND PEACE

I [Matt] was getting ready for band camp prior to my freshman year of high school. Although I wanted to be in the marching band, I wanted no part of going away for a week to camp. It was required, however, so I had to go. The morning of camp, I was not happy, and my mother noticed. As we were preparing my lunch in the kitchen, she provided some much-needed comfort. She encouraged me by listening. There was nothing to fix. She knew I needed this experience away so quitting to avoid camp was not an option. Her encouragement and the comfort she provided helped me through that first day or two until my experience at camp took over. As it turned out, the four weeks at camp each August were close to the best four weeks of my high school experience. I likely cried at the beginning because I did not want to go, but I cried at the end in my senior year because it was over and I did not want to leave.

This chapter has been written repeatedly. It has caused many disagreements, misunderstandings, and intense fellowship. That's interesting, given that the subject of the chapter is about effective understanding and peace. Both of us are passionate about the content and want the correct message to be conveyed. The truth is that the journey to an effective relationship does require hard work, and the willingness to dive into some intense fellowship.

Have you ever heard a great sermon or even a great piece of advice, one where you think, *I definitely need to put this into practice?* Jesus was not only the master of a great sermon, we find him in John 4 living it out in a practical way. Jesus gave us an example, flipping the script on the ordinary narrative. He shows how to break our historic pattern of ineffective communication.

John 4 has the story of the woman at the well. We find Jesus at the start of the story telling His disciples that He needed to go to Samaria. He really could have gone around rather than to go through Samaria. However, He was on a mission and there was a specific conversation He knew He needed to have. Jesus was tired as the story began so He sat down at the well while the disciples went to buy lunch. He didn't allow His fatigue or hunger to keep Him from the conversation.

As we look at Jesus' example, you might think how often you have been tired and hungry at the end of a day, weighed down by any number of concerns. You can still choose to enter into a conversation for the purpose of ministering to your spouse. This will often be a blessing for you as well. But let's continue to look at the woman at the well. The fact that Jesus was talking to her at all was unheard of. It was countercultural and showed the type of radical love that motivated Jesus. We, too, can choose to love in ways that are unexpected and sincere.

Jesus started this conversation by asking for a drink. He used this conversation to reach out to the woman about her deeper need. The woman was suspicious. She did not want to engage. She came specifically to the well at midday to avoid people and, of course, judgment. Sound familiar? Sometimes, we are unwilling to participate in a conversation that dives deep. As such, the woman tried to argue and get out of the conversation.

The Samaritan woman said to Him, "You are a Jew and I am a Samaritan woman. How can you ask me for a drink? (For Jews do not associate with Samaritans.)" Jesus, however, did not take offense, but continued to press in. As He continued to question her, He also gave her answers, identifying "everything that she ever did." Jesus already knew about the circumstances of her past. If you want an effective relationship with your spouse, you need to actively seek out opportunities to understand their past as well as their present.

Then it's important that we listen and clarify each other's understanding and assumptions of what is being said during the conversation. The woman said something that was factually true but not completely honest: "I have no husband." Jesus acknowledged that she was not married, seeking to explore her relationships because they were a prime influence in how she interacted in the moment. Jesus wanted to help her understand her needs.

What can we learn from Jesus here to help us in our marriage communication challenges? For one, asking questions and truly listening to the response helps us gain more understanding. Jesus didn't focus on the half-truth she uttered and responded calmly, "You are right when you say you have no husband." His words encouraged her to go beyond the half-truth to engage the full truth. The man before her was no ordinary man, and this was no ordinary conversation. He answered her and that exchange led to the resolution she needed. She could express her true need, a relationship with the Savior, which she didn't consciously know she had prior to the talk with Jesus.

Resolution provides the comfort that is needed for growth, both individually and in the relationship. It is tempting to resolve an issue or conflict on the surface. Digging deeper resulted in a more complete healing and understanding. Focused conversation keeps us in our specific roles as speaker and listener, which leads to a more effective outcome.

Keep in mind that resolution is driven by the needs of the speaker. The speaker that has a better understanding of what they need will more effectively say what comfort or resolution will look like for them. The listener can then provide the comfort the speaker needs now. This creates future patterns that provide an incentive for more positive experiences.

The listener may not be able to agree with every request. The solution may require more collaboration, but isn't that the point? We seek to have real conversations with one another in the hope of finding comfort and healing. We often tell couples that this is an opportunity to bless the other party, to put our own needs and wants on hold to comfort them. The beauty of this approach is we can know that our spouse will be able to reciprocate as we have more intentional conversations.

There are times when what the speaker is asking for to be comforted is triggering to the listener. Jesus set aside His needs throughout His ministry, we should be willing to follow His lead. In John 15:13, we read, "Greater love has no one than this: to lay down one's life for one's friends." Take the time to reverse the roles of speaker and listener to find a better understanding of any resistance.

You might say, "This was all well and good for Jesus. He was perfect, but you don't know my spouse." You might even try to hide the truth about yourself, like the woman at the well. "You don't really know who I am." We have often felt unknown, unworthy, and unlovable in these conversations. We have made mistakes, at times making things worse. The solution we are offering is one of honesty. These conversations, while not always easy, are necessary in getting below the surface to the heart of the matter. There is much fruit in using the tools and techniques we have outlined. It takes practice, practice, and more practice. These conversations become easier with time, as you both allow one another to go through the process of being seen and known.

Anger is one of the most prevalent emotions we all experience. What we see on the surface when someone is angry goes much deeper. We are angry but there are other emotions that drive the anger. We will explore that next.

MARRIAGE MATTERS TOOLS FOR CHAPTER 24

Think about a life event that has caused stress regularly from the past. Take some time to think about how your reaction is different from your spouse's.

1. Describe to your spouse the issue that is causing the stress. Your spouse's behavior may be a part. It is okay to acknowledge that, but the focus is on your pain. Don't blame or complain.
2. Do you need to give up your right to be right?
3. Is forgiveness needed for insisting on having your own way?
4. Acknowledge that the source of the pain may be in the past, but your spouse is experiencing that pain in the present.
5. What are the emotions that are causing you to want to defend or minimize your spouse's pain?
6. What boundaries can be set to change future interactions?

EVALUATE YOUR PROGRESS

1. What did you learn about your spouse?

2. What did you learn about your own emotions and perspective?

3. Are you motivated to do this again with another topic?

DIGGING DEEPER INTO CHAPTER 24

This chapter's Word search is
sacrifice

Hebrews 13:16

John 15:13

Psalm 51:17

Romans 5:8

CHAPTER 25

CONFRONTING ANGER

When I [Matt] was growing up, Friday nights had some of the best television, particularly at 8:00 p.m. *The Incredible Hulk* was "can't miss tv." We did not have the ability to record back then, so if I was not home, I did not get to see the episode. What's more, there were no streaming services so I could watch it later or multiple times. Although he tried hard not to be, David Bruce Banner would eventually be triggered and lose control of his ability to handle the anger he had inside. He would then Hulk out and much damage would ensue. Of course, as the hero in the story, his anger would often save the day.

In the long-term development of the Hulk character, Bruce eventually did learn to control and use his anger for good. The question then is, can you? If you ever want to grow more deeply in your marriage, or grow individually, write a book with your spouse. My husband and I had some words and intense times of fellowship over

193

writing and editing this book. He and I have different writing styles, different approaches, priorities, and perspectives. The discussions we have had initially have been a little higher in volume and a lot more intense than we have had previously to writing the book.

We thought that we had been doing well, but the Lord was about to make us dig deeper. After all, we had arrived, and our experiences were so good that we thought it would be a good idea to write a book on marriage. There's the rub. Writing a book on marriage has caused us to turn over new rocks, find more scary things under them, and open up more need for more conversations. By writing, we were opening the proverbial can of worms in our marriage. However, we do know that in opening this can of worms, we now can eventually come to the bottom of the can.

I [Ellen] heard a sermon recently that talked about a pastor's problem with anxiety. He said that dealing with anxiety was his thing. He could pray about it, quote Scripture, confess it, and have people hold him accountable. This issue, he believed, would be a part of his DNA until he stood before Jesus in heaven. It is true we do need to learn to bring all our emotions to God who can help us deal with them appropriately. However, what struck me about this sermon is how this pastor believed it was his "thing."

The pastor did not stop there, but he reminded us that while it may not be anxiety, we all have a "thing," that is, the universal human sinful condition that causes us all to struggle in some area. Recognizing who we are is never an excuse to say, "This is just who I am" or worse, "You knew this about me when you married me, so you will just have to deal with it." This is one of the points at which our marriages will continue to struggle, if we allow it.

I [Ellen] would say that I am an emotional person. I made my living as a doula, a support person for women giving birth. I provided comfort and a calming influence for people in highly emotional, intense situations. In this role, I was their emotional touchstone as well as their physical support. When I am at home, however, I felt that I could let my guard down. That is, I could be myself, and often that came with angry outbursts. I felt the need to defend myself and to explain why my actions were justified.

The ways in which anger expresses itself varies. Anger can be holding a grudge, sarcasm, holding emotions in and then exploding, taking offense, along with others. We have seen and heard these on social media, in movies, pop culture songs, etc. The one thing I have learned over the last several years is that anger is often a front. If we examine what is going on underneath the anger, there are often deeper feelings driving that anger.

Let's look at one word which for me is a big trigger: ridiculous. This word, when used on me, will cause a big reaction. The feelings that go along with that word are betrayal, shame, hurt, and even anxiety. Pretty extreme, right? I think the answer is both yes and no. I have learned that if I bring these negative emotions to my husband, and to God, I can feel less triggered, and eventually less angry.

What is described next is an example of the downward spiral of anger. My husband and I have different personalities as you know by now. He has an approach of keeping everything on an even keel, whereas I am much more likely to wade into a problem and clear the air. That means I am more likely to argue and attempt to gain a resolution. Years ago, Matt would say, "I'm sorry you feel that way." For me, this was cause for an immediate argument. Let's look at why.

I felt that in his apology, he was not actually saying he was sorry. He was expressing regret that I had worked myself into an emotional state that was unnecessary, but ultimately, he bore no responsibility in how I felt. I was to deal with these emotions on my own. We were both operating with a lot of assumptions. Because I am an emotional person, I assumed I knew the emotional subtext in any conversation. Some of the kids even said that it was my superpower. I would allow those assumptions to fuel my anger. Because I believed my assumptions were true, I didn't dig any deeper.

My response to Matt's attempt to engage with the "I'm sorry you feel that way" approach at first caused him to be defensive. From his perspective, Matt's apology was rejected which fueled a reaction of anger in him. So the downward cycle would continue. "I'm sorry you feel that way" meant that Matt was dumping the situation on me and leaving me to fend for myself. I would feel hurt and have no way of receiving comfort or healing. Matt was not providing what I needed which would make me angrier. Matt's justification would do nothing to solve my anger.

It was true Matt could feel sorry that I felt that way. However, I needed an apology but what I got was deflection, causing a larger divide. All I wanted in that situation was to be seen and heard. Matt's evasiveness made me angrier because he refused to be present with me in my pain. That caused additional resistance and a desire to go back into Matt's all-too-familiar pattern of being "right" and avoiding an emotional situation rather than addressing it in a way that could lead to healing.

Apologizing puts people in a vulnerable position emotionally, which often makes them uncomfortable. Being uncomfortable then leads to them not apologizing as often as they should. We needed to break the cycle of being uncomfortable. What do we do if we don't feel sorry about the anger our spouse is experiencing? Is it possible that he did not do or say something offensive? The temptation is to want to stay in our mentality that we are always right, that our partner is the one with the problem. It is a good thing that Jesus did not insist on His right to be right. He could have stayed in His anger, but instead He chose to serve. Now that's what He's directing us to do. We must understand our anger but also be motivated by love to address it.

There are many biblical lessons on anger. We will detail some later in this chapter, but the first one we want to highlight is from Philippians 4:8, in which Paul first talked about whatever is true, whatever is noble, etc. In making assumptions about your spouse, you are not asking yourself what is true. When you pause there and ask if the assumptions (yours or theirs) are true, you will make many improvements to your marriage.

Through James in the first chapter of his letter, the Lord says, "Everyone should be quick to listen, slow to speak and slow to become angry, because human anger does not produce the righteousness that God desires" (James 1:19-20). Most people who have been Christians for any length of time recognize that passage and even offer up an "amen." Yet, like Bruce Banner's Hulk, we let our anger get to the point of no return. After we express our rage and feel better, we relax and return to our pre-Hulk form, either with tattered clothes or mostly naked. Underneath, that shame stays with us until the next episode.

Studying biblical anger is an interesting pursuit and can be confusing. God gets angry and has some intense responses, but in all of that, He does not sin. He even tells us in Ephesians not to allow our anger to turn to sin. So if that is the case, we have a justification for Hulking out in anger, especially if we are going to be the hero and save our spouse from certain doom.

For Bruce, getting triggered and becoming the Hulk was a cover and prevented him from dealing with the emotion underneath the anger. Allowing ourselves to get angry is a great way not to have to deal with the truth. It is much safer because the anger puts up a wall that enables us to blame others and keep people out. The rampage and even the physical force might work when you are younger. Using anger as an adult, however, gets us in more trouble. The wall that hides or seals us off does not work well in adult relationships, especially in marriage.

What can we do when our anger threatens our relationship? Here are two that come to mind:

"A hot-tempered person stirs up conflict, but the one who is patient calms a quarrel" (Proverbs 15:18).

"But you, O Lord, are a God merciful and gracious, slow to anger and abounding in steadfast love and faithfulness" (Psalm 86:15).

If you want to minimize the impact of anger, don't answer harshly. Proverbs 15:1 advises, "A gentle answer turns away wrath, but a harsh word stirs up anger." And Paul wrote, "Finally brothers, whatever is true, whatever is noble, whatever is right, whatever is pure, whatever is lovely, whatever is admirable, if anything is excellent or praiseworthy, think about these things" (Philippians 4:8).

"I am sorry, I was wrong, will you forgive me?" is much more effective. Even if you were not the one who was wrong, apologizing by saying "I'm sorry you feel that way" often is the wrong approach.

As we move forward to the end of this book, it seems that a pattern has developed in acknowledging the roadblocks and how we address them. There is good news in that we address each of our roadblocks in a similar way. We can build on what we learn when engaging the "easy" offenses and use that experience when the more difficult and deeper wounds need to be addressed. That pattern is a good thing. We can more easily recognize a pattern than random acts.

We have said this earlier, and we will likely write it again: Listen to understand, not to critique or change. Speak to be known not to blame. Doing both lowers your defenses and helps your spouse to be more open. It builds trust when the downward spiral reverses itself and moves upward. Once we were able to make changes in some of the lighter topics or perspectives that did not set off a volcanic reaction, we are more prepared to address those Mount Everests in our relationship.

Part of dealing with any stress is to be able to submit to one another. Doing so disarms our defenses and opens communication that accomplishes what we desire. Submission goes both ways in a relationship. However, submission that is one-sided is not submission at all. Let's look at that in the next chapter.

MARRIAGE MATTERS TOOLS FOR CHAPTER 25

The goal here is to recognize the underlying emotions and unfulfilled expectations in our anger.

1. What is something in your relationship that causes anger?
2. What are the assumptions that are driving the reaction?
3. Once you feel understood, determine what you need.
4. Repeat #1 but reverse the roles with your spouse.

EVALUATE YOUR PROGRESS

1. What did you learn about your spouse?

2. What did you learn about your own emotions and perspective?

3. Are you motivated to do this again with another topic?

DIGGING DEEPER INTO CHAPTER 25

This chapter's Word search is
anger

James 1:20

Psalm 37:8

Proverbs 14:29

Ecclesiastes 10:4

CHAPTER 26

SUBMISSION

One of our greatest struggles was believing that things would get better if only the other person would change. Years ago, we got our very first minivan. This was something that previously would have been out of our price range. However, the circumstances of getting that minivan involved a car accident and a settlement. This was a blessing in disguise as we found ourselves able to take care of some needs in our home. We had three children at the time and the minivan made all the difference.

A few years after that, my husband decided that he would like to sell the minivan. I did not want to sell the minivan, feeling that it was the only good thing we owned, and selling it would only put us further behind. I felt that if we were to buy another minivan, we would only be buying others' problems, and furthermore, the mini-van, a Honda Odyssey, was reliable and stylish, certainly worth more to us than its trade in value.

Matt and I struggled during this time, each feeling that the other was not listening. When I first became Christian, and as a relatively new bride, I knew the value and importance of submission. I would talk to anyone who would listen about the beauty and value of submission. It is never about the person in front of us ("submit to one another out of reverence for Christ") but about the God who loves us and is asking us to do the submitting.

Where the van was concerned, however, I had no interest in laying aside my concerns. In fact, the opposite was true. I reminded my husband that both our names were on the title, and I had no intention of selling the Odyssey, so he could just fight me. After what seemed like months, Matt tried a different approach. He came to me and asked me to pray about this situation. He had me right there. At this point in our marriage, submission was so much a part of my DNA, I did not have much of a choice. I still did not want to pray. I did not want to do as my husband asked, much less ask God to intervene because I did not want Him to take Matt's side. In this moment, I submitted myself to my husband, but, more importantly, I submitted my heart to God. With gritted teeth and white knuckles, I came to Him.

I asked God to show me His thoughts on this situation. God, as He often does, did something surprising. He asked me to release this to Matt's control, to allow Matt to take the lead. He did not say we should sell the van; He did not say we should keep it. He asked me to let it go and submit it to my husband. I told my husband that God had asked me to release this situation. I thanked Matt for his loving care of all of us, and his oversight of the finances. That was it. It was a no-strings-attached release, because I had trusted my husband and God who had asked me. We ended up keeping the van.

How do we lovingly confront our spouse? The first thing that comes to mind as I was thinking through our experience was submission. When we got married, the pastor preached a message based on Ephesians 5, at my [Ellen's] request. Our dear friend and pastor briefly addressed me, and then turned his full attention in a rather fiery sermon on my soon-to-be husband. The same passage in Ephesians that asks a wife to be submissive to her husband commands the husband to lay down his life for his wife, to love her as Christ loves the church. This would be tough for any husband, but that is not actually the point. So, in this very misunderstood passage,

God encourages both partners to extend themselves to do what may not come naturally to benefit the relationship.

The first command is to submit to one another out of reverence for Christ. Paul wrote in Ephesians 5:21-25,

Submit to one another out of reverence for Christ. Wives, submit yourselves to your own husbands as you do to the Lord. For the husband is the head of the wife as Christ is the head of the church, his body, of which he is the Savior. Now as the church submits to Christ, so also wives should submit to their husbands in everything. Husbands, love your wives, just as Christ loved the church and gave himself up for her.

Submission is a matter of laying down your own wants and tendencies for the good of the one in front of you. When you consider that Jesus did that, it does not seem such a hard thing. Jesus also said, "Greater love hath no man than this, that he lay down his life for his friends" (John 15:13, KJV).

A quick overview of Jesus' life reveals that He lived a different life than He is asking of His bride, the Church. His self-sacrifice was rooted completely in submission to the will of the Father. Looking at the role of the husband, both sacrifice and submission are required. The wife's role has both components too, but in a different order. The wife sacrifices her desires to submit; the husband submits to sacrifice for his wife.

The Lord knew in the Garden that submission would be difficult for the wife, just as sacrifice would be a challenge for the husband. When I [Matt] don't sacrifice my desires, things in relationships get out of whack just as much, if not more, than when my wife does not submit. Ultimately, we both are responsible for our own role when we don't meet the standard. The Lord knows in advance where our greatest struggle will occur and addresses that struggle not with a hammer but as a loving call to be a blessing to one another.

Most of the public discussion about submission is focused on women submitting to men. Doing so offers an incomplete picture. Let's look at what the Bible says about submission and how it benefits a marriage.

1. Hebrews 13:17 states, "Have confidence in your leaders and submit to their authority, because they

keep watch over you as those who must give an account. Do this so that their work will be a joy, not a burden, for that would be of no benefit to you." When we submit, we make work easier for those to whom we submit. That is true of leaders in government and leadership in the home.

Since each partner has areas in which they lead in the relationship, the application for this is not just focused in one direction. We can avoid escalating arguments when we submit to our partner's desire. That does not mean we become a doormat. Having to only submit one way will lead to frustration and dysfunction in the long run. Resentment builds up in one partner and then eventually will explode.

2. James 4:7 says, "Submit yourselves, then, to God. Resist the devil, and he will flee from you." The marital relationship is a major focus for Satan and his crew. Submission thwarts Satan's strategy to drive a wedge between the husband and wife in a marital relationship.

3. Titus 2:5 states, "To be self-controlled and pure, to be busy at home, to be kind, and to be subject to their husbands, so that no one will malign the word of God." Submission helps promote ministry to others.

I [Matt] had a conversation with a friend who recognized a pattern of behavior that occurred when they were going on a trip. It was not something that happened every day but the dance was predictable when it did. We all have expectations about that stress inducing time. Some of us drop everything and go an hour before. Others start a week in advance, lining up clothes and suitcases in our living space that we trip over ten times before leaving. Which is the correct approach? This is one question where there is not a right or wrong answer. We just have our perspectives about how our expectations influence the coming exchange.

How is something that is supposed to be fun a cause for fighting and quarreling? Rather than not say anything, my friend proactively set a boundary prior to the triggering event, and it worked.

He did not point fingers or criticize their failures of the past, but set boundaries on what he wanted and shared them. Rather than fight all the way there, they had a positive time building together. They had a similar conversation prior to the trip home as well. In addition to the success of that trip they now have a template and a positive experience on which to base future trips. They can begin a pattern of positive interactions that will build into their relationship rather than add additional strife.

As we can see from the outcome of this story, when we take the time to understand and submit our desires in favor of our spouse, our pattern of engagement can change dramatically. After the fact, the solution seems so obvious and easy. Submission can be difficult, but it helps us reach what we wanted in the first place. In this case a stress-free trip where we can build positively into our relationship.

In a world where people struggle to understand and apply submission, the question becomes: How do we impact a world that seems to reject it? That world might be initially limited to our spouses or our kids. The good news is that we can motivate others by modeling what Jesus teaches us. When you model it before your spouse, your spouse will be more willing to model it for you. The doormat turns into a revolving door of each one returning the blessing. As you model this for your children, your future sons- and daughters-in-law will thank you for it. The more you can mentor positive patterns in their lives, the better equipped they will be in their relationships. Let's move on now to our next chapter and look at how we can pass on what we have learned and motivate others to join us.

MARRIAGE MATTERS TOOLS FOR CHAPTER 26

As we come toward the end of this book, we want to put everything together. The big picture fix to all the tools we have recommended involves submission. Prayer can give us some much-needed perspective and makes submission easier.

It is easy to assume that if only your spouse would change, then things would be better. Now that you have a better understanding of your spouse's perspective, your next growth step is to submit and work to help heal and meet their needs. This can be difficult. It is the final step that you take to grow yourself and your relationship with our spouse and Jesus.

Ask questions so you can transform your assumptions to experience knowledge and truth.

Ask your spouse what their top struggle is. Do you know your own? Ask that as well.

Use the previously-learned tools of effective listening and speaking to engage in a new conversation. Those will help you find the answer together with your spouse.

Anticipate that you will run into resistance. Don't give in to the temptation to go back to old patterns of defending and fixing.

Did your spouse answer the way you think they would?

If they did not, then keep going until you understand the different perspectives. Comfort and peace do not necessarily come with changing your perspective but with understanding each other's.

1. Commit to pray specifically for that area a few times a week.

DIGGING DEEPER INTO CHAPTER 26

This chapter's Word search is
prayer

Matthew 6:33

Matthew 18:19

Romans 15:5-6

Psalm 122:6

CHAPTER 27

CHANGING THE PATTERN

Many will say that marriage is under attack in most societies. There is no doubt that is true. The body of believers is willing to point their fingers of blame to bring light on the attack. As we have seen though, our greatest challenge is not "out there," but is in our own marriages. What if we were to work on being a better example as married Christians rather than focusing on what is "wrong" with "them"? What price are we willing to pay to make our marriage all God intends for it to be? The Lord does the healing. We need to give Him the time and allow Him to give us the tools. We need to be willing to learn and set aside our own desires and serve each other. We also need to be intentional about time invested, our communication skills, and our efforts to listen and understand as we have discussed throughout the book.

Many years ago, Matt attended a men's conference. He was gone for most of the weekend, meaning that I was also left at home with young kids. I was rather irritated that he was gone for so long. While I understood the benefits, I was about to get a real wake up call.

Matt came home and said we had to talk. This caused an extremely defensive reaction in me, and I was in fight-or-flight mode. In fact, I was not at all sure I was planning to stay in the conversation. I was pouty and angry and sarcastic. Then something happened. He took my hands and got on his knees. His eyes filled with tears and his voice teetered with emotion. For Matt's even-tempered personality, this was nothing that I would have expected.

To be honest, I was thrilled to the core. Matt had been told to go home and apologize to his wife. It might seem that I had a list, right there and then, of things that he should apologize for, and that he was just ticking off the boxes on my clipboard. The truth, however, was something else entirely. I don't remember what he apologized for. I don't recall at the time what I might have wanted an apology for. I only remember him drawing close to me and humbling himself before me. I was extremely energized by this position of humility and vulnerability. This is what I remember all these years later. In our marriage, we have the power to enact an incredible change, if we are willing to be humble before our spouse.

We have talked through the book about how we change the pattern in our marriage. We are looking to share what God has shown us so that more patterns can change. Our official mission statement for creating Marriage House Ministries, for which this book is one of the source materials, is to provide resources that support and enhance marital and other significant relationships. Marriage House Ministries is a non-profit ministry created for the purpose of providing resources to churches who need help providing material for their congregations on the topic of marriage and to individuals looking for resources to help break lifelong patterns.

It is our goal in Marriage House Ministries to build communities of believers, have some great food and fun fellowship and prayer, and to look inwardly to better understand the reasons why we respond and react the way we do. As this occurs, it will bring dramatic transformation to us and our relationships.

Once you have been on this journey, we encourage you to go back and walk others through it too. The first motivation to continue this ministry is because God wants to have an amazing relationship with you. He is desperately and passionately interested in knowing you and you Him. He knows you perfectly but that does not mean He has a relationship with you. When setting His plan in motion, the primary example He used to help us understand was marriage as seen in Genesis 2:24 "Therefore a man shall leave his father and his mother and hold fast to his wife, and they shall become one flesh."

It is interesting that this statement was made by God before the Fall. Up to that event, Adam and Eve were perfect creatures. They had unhindered access to the Lord as He dwelt with them in the Garden of Eden. Genesis 2:25 takes the relationship a step further: "Adam and his wife were both naked, and they felt no shame." That is intimacy like no other. There is something that we needed in each other that we did not get through our fellowship with Him. God set up a primary relationship between a man and a woman for a purpose, not only to reflect the relationship between Christ and the Church but to give us so much more here on earth.

As we got started, we read books, all of which were good. When we had finished facilitating our first "How We Love" class, the wonderful couple mentoring us had left as they said they would. As typically happens in longer classes, attendance dipped after the holiday break. We finished the class with one couple and then Covid hit. Circumstances did not look good for us to continue but God had other plans. We should know by now that the Lord works in His ways and timing.

We could not meet in person during the pandemic, and we did not have a format or the technical know-how to run a class online. We contacted Milan and Kay Yerkovich, the authors of *How We Love,* who had an online option in the works. They did, however, have a DVD series that had nine videos along with some discussion questions. We got the approval of our church and a brief lesson on how to Zoom, and we were ready. Nervous but willing to step out in faith, we had several classes in a row that only had a few or only one couple. The Lord asked us to continue, so we did.

During that journey, He showed us what He was doing even when there was only one couple per class. That perspective of wanting big numbers lacked the faith we needed. At the end of one of the classes, one participant said to us, "if Jesus were here, He would say, 'Well done, good and faithful servant.'" I [Matt] thought, *well done?* That helped me see my value through the Lord's eyes. He was preparing us for ministering and making a difference in marriages. This book and other work He is doing are building a ministry to do His work in relationships.

We were not too far along in a new class when a young couple contacted us and wanted to be in a class. After some prayer, we decided to have a one-on-one class with them. We ultimately had the privilege of going to their wedding. We had a conversation that I [Matt] will never forget. First, what an amazing blessing and privilege it was to be part of their specific journey from newly-dating to marriage. Then the bride said to us during their reception that has become the primary reason we do what we do: "You and *How We Love* gave us all the tools we needed."

Our calling is to give couples the tools and perspectives to have Christ-honoring, committed, and obedient relationships with each other. Recently, we went to a celebration of life for a fellow brother in Christ, attending to support his wife. The Lord also spoke to us through her words: "Matt, thank you. We learned so much about each other." Whether at the beginning or the end of our relationship, it was an amazing place to be in ministry—helping others to know and be in relationship. It is our prayer that you will join us in this ministry by passing on what you have learned.

Titus 2:1-10 gives some calls as a challenge to share what the Lord has given to us:

> You, however, must teach what is appropriate to sound doctrine. Teach the older men to be temperate, worthy of respect, self-controlled, and sound in faith, in love and in endurance. Likewise, teach the older women to be reverent in the way they live, not to be slanderers or addicted to much wine, but to teach what is good. Urge the younger women to love their husbands and children, Be self-controlled and pure, to be busy at home, to be kind, and to be subject to their husbands, so that no one will malign the word of God. Similarly, encourage the young men to be self-controlled. In everything, set them an example by doing what is good. In your teaching shows integrity and seriousness. Soundness of speech cannot be condemned, so those who oppose you may be ashamed because they have nothing bad to say about us. Teach slaves to be subject

to their masters in everything, to try to please them, not to talk back to them. Do not steal from them, but to show that they can be fully trusted, so that in every way they will make the teaching about God our Savior attractive.

Matthew 11:28 says, "Come to me, all you who are weary and burdened, and I will give you rest." Second Corinthians 1:4 says, "He comforts us in all our afflictions, so that we may be able to comfort those who are in any affliction, with the comfort with which we ourselves are comforted by God."

God in His perfection is an emotional being and we are created in the image of God. Our emotions are marred by sin, but according to Scripture, we get our emotions from Him. When we are willing to look, they are a window into the heart of the Father. We have seen firsthand that healing after decades of resistance comes not only from logic and doctrinal truth but also from understanding and experiencing the truth that emotions show us. Both are important. Understanding our emotions can make understanding the facts easier to grasp. That process can be scary and intimidating, but we should want more understanding and growth. We are seeing it personally and with others. It works when we take the time to understand, not logically pull out a Scripture and advise others to just do it. We as a couple tried for 30 years to focus on truth and very little changed.

Understanding our emotions and applying them through love has completely changed our outlook. In truth, doing so fulfills our initial desire for logic and obedience. We see and understand Scripture more clearly than we ever have. Obedience and the process of sanctification have accelerated. Emotions don't change the truth, but we see the truth more clearly now that we understand our emotions. Our culture has elevated emotions over truth. That is not our or the biblical perspective. Our perspective is that emotion and truth work hand in hand equally. It is understandable that when emotions are out of balance, logic and "just do it because God said" do not work. Why? Because God gave us truth in Scripture and created us with the need to engage emotionally with one another— as well as to understand theology.

The very foundation of the Gospel is based on the emotions of the Father. He gave up everything and Jesus endured a literal hell for us because He desperately loves us. His purpose is not casual. "I think I would like time with my people." His responses are perfect and filled with intense emotions. Apart from love, compassion, care, and belonging, the Gospel makes very little sense. People treat God poorly or ignore Him, yet He has done and will do anything to fellowship with us except force us to love Him. That's not because He isn't powerful enough but because doing so would destroy the relationship He desired in the first place.

Has it been a while since you asked Him to be a part of your life? Perhaps you never have before? Is there something in your emotional experience that is holding you back? Do you feel unloved or unworthy? We would encourage you to take the time right now to reach out to Him. Your emotions, like ours, are messy. He is okay with that. Give Him another chance to bring healing and comfort into your life. *Jesus gave everything for you.* All He wants of you is to believe. Eternal life does not start when your life here on earth ends, but it is happening right now. Once you have accepted His invitation of faith, He will take you on a journey that will be life changing.

He does not want you to miss out on abundant joy and other positive emotions that are part of the experience God intends. Second Corinthians 9:8 says, "And God is able to bless you abundantly, so that in all things at all times, having all that you need, you will abound in every good work."

The Bible says that when we get to heaven, God will wipe away our tears. That act will bring everlasting peace, joy, comfort, and perfect fellowship for eternity. He has given us an ability to start that tear-drying process while we are here on earth when we apply the truth of Scripture to our stress, emotions, and relationship expectations.

MARRIAGE MINISTRY TOOLS FOR CHAPTER 27

This last tool is an easy one—well, sort of. The challenge is to take what you have learned and share it with others. Perhaps you have some friends or family members that would be blessed by a different perspective in their relationships. After reading the final chapter, share this and be a blessing to others by purchasing them a copy of the book. Throughout our lives when others have been generous with us, they would say that we needed to pay it forward.

Go back and regularly re-read the tools and commit to regularly engaging your spouse to understand. Create a plan to set aside some regular time to work on these principles.

LOVE IS . . .

We made it through 27 chapters of a book on marriage, and we have not looked at what is commonly known as the love chapter. That chapter and a few others are a great way to end our book.

Our new way of communicating has led to a more complete understanding and obedience to many parts of Scripture. We see each other, truth, and the Lord Jesus more clearly. This is something we never could have done alone nor without a clearer picture of who we are now because of how our past shaped us. One of those passages is Colossians 3:5-10:

> Put to death, therefore, whatever belongs to your earthly nature: sexual immorality, impurity, lust, evil desires and greed, which is idolatry. Because of these, the wrath of God is coming. You used to walk in these ways, in the life you once lived. But now you must also rid yourselves of all such things as these: anger, rage, malice, slander, and filthy language from your lips. Do not lie to each other, since you have taken off your old self with its practices and have put on the new self, which is being renewed in knowledge in the image of its Creator.

We have been able to help each other put to death the things that are destructive and keep us away from each other and the Lord. Lying is so much more than just telling someone something that is factually inaccurate. We can share the truth with each other and the Lord more fully.

Colossians 3:12-15 looks at what we can accomplish together, not perfectly of course, but with enough frequency that we experience all the things listed more fully.

> Therefore, as God's chosen people, holy and dearly loved, clothe yourselves with compassion, kindness, humility, gentleness and patience. Bear with each other and forgive

one another if any of you has a grievance against someone. Forgive as the Lord forgave you. And over all these virtues put on love, which binds them all together in perfect unity. Let the peace of Christ rule in your hearts, since as members of one body you were called to peace. And be thankful.

We are eternally thankful that the Lord has taken us through this journey. We will close with our final Bible verse coming from 1 Corinthians 13:4–13:

Love is patient, love is kind. It does not envy, it does not boast, it is not proud. It does not dishonor others, it is not self-seeking, it is not easily angered, it keeps no record of wrongs. Love does not delight in evil but rejoices with the truth. It always protects, always trusts, always hopes, always perseveres. Love never fails. But where there are prophecies, they will cease; where there are tongues, they will be stilled; where there is knowledge, it will pass away. For we know in part and we prophesy in part, but when completeness comes, what is in part disappears. When I was a child, I talked like a child, I thought like a child, I reasoned like a child. When I became a man, I put the ways of childhood behind me. For now we see only a reflection as in a mirror; then we shall see face to face. Now I know in part; then I shall know fully, even as I am fully known. And now these three remain: faith, hope and love. But the greatest of these is love.

Our perspective and our communication with each other are now characterized by patience and kindness. It does not envy or boast. We are not proud. We do not dishonor each other. We seek to understand each other rather than be angry. The record of wrongs from our past are continuing to be wiped clean. We don't rejoice in being right or having our perspective "win" but in the joy of truly knowing each other. We now look to protect each other, build trust and support each other to persevere through the challenges that our lives offer. Through this passage as the verses suggest, we are now able to put our childhood ways of relationship that don't work as adults behind us.

We close by summarizing what we wrote throughout the

book. The Lord created us to bond with others, which is indispens-
able for emotional, physical, and spiritual health and development.
We are needy people. That is not a bad thing because those needs
drive us to relationship with others and ultimately to God. Marriage
is one of the ways the Lord demonstrates the intimacy He desires
with us. However, sin comes into play and messes with that plan.

*The two greatest challenges in marriage are how we manage
stress and the expectations we have of ourselves and our spouse.
The best way to handle stress and expectations is to understand
our emotions—how and why they operate and what we can
expect when they are healed and under the Lordship of Christ—
through a biblical lens. We engage them to find comfort and healing through sharing with our spouse.*

Many of us have spent a lifetime either avoiding emotions or
controlling our situations so we don't have to deal with them. Some
don't have a vocabulary for emotions. If we can't understand or acknowledge what is happening inside us, it makes sense that we would
want to blame the other person in the relationship. Some can perhaps
logically and intellectually describe our emotions, but that is much
different than feeling them, owning them, and understanding how
they are impacting our experience either positively or negatively.

There are many roadblocks to intimacy which we create
through a lack of understanding of how we are to relate to one
another. Our understanding changes when we intentionally look
further into what motivates us to react or respond as we do and
discover God's plan for how we should respond. It is much easier
to react than it is to respond. Our verbal and non-verbal memories
teach us patterns of behavior that often create more challenges than
they address. Many of us don't have verbal memories when we start
this journey.

When you trust Him, the Lord will provide what is needed for healing and comfort when you are ready to handle them.
You want to be right and point your finger and shout, "It's your
fault, not mine!" You assume and conclude that if only your spouse
would change, things would be better. You allow yourself to rein-
force learned behaviors that result in nagging each other with the
same complaints while expecting things to change. *They just need to
hear the same thing I have said a thousand times, once more and everything
will be better.* You allow judgment to replace seeking to understand.

We are praying that Jesus helps you see others through His eyes which will lead to a 180-degree perspective change. It is possible to get that loving feeling back that you had when you first started dating your spouse. Getting those positive feelings back are a blessing that the Lord wants to bestow on you, if you let Him. Part of the journey to get there is to have honest conversations about how you feel and how those emotions are impacting you. You must understand that the challenges from your spouse's reactions are generally not the issue. Marriage gives you an opportunity to help in some of God's most important work, which is to be an example of the relationship that Jesus has with His Church. When you relate to others properly, you better understand how to run the race of sanctification in Jesus. You also need to understand that you are to proactively take responsibility to provide the comfort your spouse needs to grow.

You can confront anger more effectively when you engage it rather than give into it or bury it, when you understand its source and then submit to one another. Often the best way to learn is to teach others. Remember that this is an ongoing journey, not a one-and-done moment. Your needs and histories are deep. They also change constantly throughout your life. God has a lesson for you and He teaches you through understanding your history while bonding with others so that you can more effectively bond with Him.

If there is one thing to remember when you are in the heat of an intense discussion is that *the needs that are motivating and driving your partner's reaction are often the same needs that are motivating and driving yours.* So if you are arguing with your spouse, then ultimately you are fighting something in yourself. Sounds silly to fight about the same thing, right? Well, sort of. Now that you can recognize the existence of certain triggers in yourself and your spouse, the struggle can be changed to a discussion where listening and sharing leads to growth, understanding, and healing.

Our perspective when we complain, nag, and engage in avoidance has changed. We have come to understand that when we "complain" or avoid, it is not an attack on each other. Because we are not taking it personally, not trying to talk each other out of our feelings, or demonstrating that the other is "wrong" or I am "right,". We can provide comfort and understanding at the time of the discussion rather than holding it in. That changes the patterns we have learned that fueled our conflict. The foundation for those patterns is different for each of us, but our patterns are understandable and predictable. Therefore, there are predictable solutions.

What we used to see as irrational and immature in each other, we now see as logical and understandable. It makes sense to me why I react the way I do. It makes sense to me why my spouse reacts the way they do. *That understanding does not completely stop the trigger, but it helps to more effectively deal with it in the moment when the trigger happens.* Understanding our emotions and what triggers them has reduced our false assumptions and unfair judgements of each other. We have built positive patterns of interaction rather than negative. We still have disagreements, but they don't linger.

Since we have started a deep dive to understand and experience our emotions, our relationships with others, and especially the Lord have grown. That emotional understanding has made it easier to accept and be obedient to what the Bible teaches. Prior to that it was a lot of white-knuckling effort. We had to grin and bear it, and we were legalistic. Now when we fall short, grace and mercy have so much more meaning to us in our relationship with each other and the Lord.

Talk with your spouse to be known. Listen to your spouse to understand.

1. What have you learned through this study about your spouse and yourself?

2. What specific truth are you going to apply to your relationship?

Throughout the course of the book, we have looked at more than 200 different verses of Scripture. One of the most important lessons we learned in this process is to take what we know and understand and experience it. Many of the Scripture verses that we have known for decades and can quote in our mind have not and did not change us—until now. Now we live and experience them through our emotions. Doing so has made those Scriptures, and our relationship come alive! Truth is good, but experiencing truth in relationship with Jesus and each other is greater. We see truth more clearly and have a fuller understanding of ourselves, each other and Jesus.

May God bless each of you on your journey. We pray that the Lord has spoken to your heart. Thank you for giving us the blessing to share His message in obedience to Him with you. If we can be of service to you, please contact us through our Facebook Marriage House Ministries page, or email us at marriagehouseministries@gmail.com.